Overexposed

Sylvère Lotringer

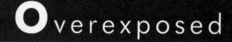

Overexposed

TREATING SEXUAL PERVERSION IN AMERICA

Pantheon Books
New York

Library of Congress Cataloging-in-Publication Data

Lotringer, Sylvère.
  Overexposed.

    1. Sex offenders—United States—Psychology.   2. Sexual deviation—
United States.   3. Sex crimes—United States.   4. Sex
therapy.   I. Title.
HQ72.U53L68   1988   616.85′83′00973   87-46056
ISBN 0-394-56170-8
ISBN 0-394-75731-9 (pbk.)

Book design by Jennifer Dossin
Manufactured in the United States of America

First Edition

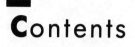

Contents

With many thanks to John Kelsey for transcribing tapes; to Andrew Mirhej for transcribing and editing some of the material; to Marshall Blonsky for his advice; to Chris Kraus for her perceptive comments and suggestions; and to my editors, David Sternbach and Ed Cohen, for their intelligence, taste, and manners.

S.L.

I discovered there was an endless source of robust enjoyment in trifling with psychiatrists . . .

—Vladimir Nabokov
Lolita

Overexposed

Mores

> "Another instrument of these pain tourists is the *signal switch* sir . . . what they call the 'yes no' sir. . . . 'I love you I hate you' at supersonic alternating speed. . . . Take orgasm noises sir and cut them in with torture and accident groans and screams sir and operating-room jokes sir and flicker sex and torture film right with it sir. . . . It would have a comic effect sir. . . ."
>
> —**William Burroughs**
> ***Nova Express***

At the end of the nineteenth century, a well-known French lawyer, M. de Rochefort, successfully defended his client, an anarchist caught red-handed with a bomb, with the following argument: "I don't deny that my client was carrying a bomb. But this doesn't prove that he was going to use it. After all, I myself always carry with me everything I'd need to commit a rape."

Bombs can be banned and handguns registered, but penises cannot be checked at the door. The problem is not just the organ, it is the impulse, the intention, the opportunity. How, then, does one deal with people's heads? How does one dissuade them from throwing around the time-bomb of their sexuality?

In 1981, while doing research for a paper on sexuality and language, I fell upon a sex clinic unlike anything I had seen before. Actually, there are still very few of its kind, a handful at most, on the whole North American continent.*

What is unusual about the treatment this clinic offers is not that it deals with sexual offenders, but *how* it deals with them. The treatment reveals as much about the perversity of modern therapeutics as it does about the nature, and possible cure, of "dangerous perversions." It does more still: it strongly suggests that what we now call "sexuality" is a strange perversion of the sexual instinct.

Sexuality is after all a recent phenomenon. It only emerged two centuries ago as a distinct body of knowledge (biology of reproduction, neuropathology of sexual aberrations, etc.) and an object of intense preoccupation. At the end of the nineteenth century, Krafft-Ebing introduced the first edition of his celebrated *Psychopathia Sexualis* in the following fashion: "Few people are conscious of the deep influence exerted by sexual life upon the sentiment, thought, and action of man in his social relations to others." Well, who could possibly say that today?

J. G. Ballard, the science-fiction writer, comes closer to home in *The Atrocity Exhibition*, in which a character raises "an interesting question—in what way is intercourse per vagina more stimulating than with this ashtray, say, or with the angle between two walls? Sex is now a

---

* The doctors, technicians, and patients who speak in this book are composites based on numerous interviews with sex therapists and patients in the United States and Canada. All names and locations of persons, institutions, and events described have been changed.

conceptual act, it's probably only in terms of the perversions that we can make contact with each other. The perversions are completely neutral, cut off from any suggestion of psychopathology—in fact, most of the ones I tried out are out of date. We need to invent a series of imaginary sexual perversions just to keep the activity alive. . . ."

Over the last two decades, thousands of sex-therapy clinics have sprung up to meet the challenge—and treat the casualties—of the new "sexual freedom." Most of these clinics are remedial in essence. They deal with sexual "dysfunctions" through an arsenal of techniques derived from the austere teachings of Masters and Johnson. Their basic axiom is a secular version of Wilhelm Reich's exalted vision of "orgastic potency" as the ultimate remedy to sexual and cultural discontent. "Orgasm therapy" is now routinely administered all over the country—and all over the Western world—as the treatment of choice for a wide range of sexual impairments, such as premature ejaculation, impotence, vaginal spasm, and failure to orgasm. In the lexicon of sex therapists, the treatment involves: gradual desensitization of traumatic situations; exploration of relational difficulties in couples; sensuality training through touching, auto- and manual stimulation; and finally, control of orgasm. Single clients are being provided with sex surrogates under the close supervision of experienced psychologists.

Kirby Dick's recent documentary film, *Private Practices*, records the lives of two men who managed to overcome their fear of women with the help of Maureen Sullivan, America's best-known surrogate. Maureen trains each man to lie down naked with her in front of mirrors, comparing anatomies ("My vagina is four and a half inches long"). She gives them "the skeleton of lovemaking," providing, along the way, emotional counseling and advice on dating. It takes three months to a year to secure impaired clients "a satisfying experience."

Wilhelm Reich's "orgasmology" wasn't simply meant to introduce consumers to the joy of sex. His was a brave attempt to counter Freud's ultimate resignation to human discontent by going to the moral and social roots of psychic inhibition. The "natural" striving for pleasure, Reich argued, is an affirmation of life; it should therefore receive "unrestricted gratification." Society, he thought, keeps repressing full sexual capacity into neurosis, or distorting it into perversion. "Only the liberation of the natural capacity for love," he concluded, "could master their sadistic destructiveness."

What became of Reich's far-reaching socioeconomic analysis of sexuality in the hands of American clinical pragmatism is a fascinating story of cross-cultural cannibalization. Throwing out the hard political edge of the orgasm theory, Masters and Johnson quickly turned "full sexual capacity" into a physiological formula. Actually Reich had exposed himself to such a cold clinical fate when, in the thirties, he set out to establish the experimental proof of his cultural intuitions. "Sexual pleasure," he wrote at the time, "has never been measured." Masters and Johnson certainly measured up to his expectations.

Reich's investigation of the bioelectrical energy on the surface of the body had led him far beyond the confines of depth psychology and physiology, into a biocosmic vision of sexual pleasure as the life process itself. The American response to his wild prophesying was more subdued. Subjected to bold lab measurements drawing on the most advanced technology, sexual pleasure froze into a forceful therapeutic strategy. Formerly a European concept charged with radical energies, orgasm had become the yardstick of healthy American middle-class adjustment.

Masters and Johnson's quiet exploration of the world of orgasm set the stage for a wider campaign fueled by greater social permissiveness and the media's insatiable demand for sensation. Like a virus let loose from the lab, sexual pleasure exploded in successive waves in the public's consciousness, creating an ever-pressing demand for pop expertise and inflated formulations. "Why be satisfied with one or two orgasms?" asks Dr. Irene Kassorla, a respected disciple of Masters and Johnson. "Among the patients who have learned and practiced my techniques," she asserts in *Nice Girls Do*, "having as many as a hundred orgasms in a two-hour period is not uncommon. Afterwards, they report, they're better able to focus into their normal activities. They feel peaceful, relaxed, and yet more energetic and ready to participate in work and family involvements. . . ."

It may well be, as many sex professionals contend, that in the privacy of their homes the American population remains mostly unaffected by this verbal escalation, and still prey to sexual inhibition. No one, however, can deny that the widespread selling of sex has drastically altered people's attitudes and expectations. The current effort to curtail the dissemination of sexual material paradoxically testifies to the overwhelming character of the phenomenon. Pop psychologists who now openly advocate orgasm as a moral duty, a categorical imperative, or, at any rate, an inalienable right written into our biological constitution, are not at variance with the basic ethos of rank-and-file sex specialists. In a fairly short time, we've come a long way from the social suppression of sex to the outpouring of signs of genital prowess.

Gone are the days when the anonymous Victorian gentleman, author of *My Secret Life*, wondered if men shared his strange "letches," hoping that his own experience, if printed, would enable others to compare notes, as he himself couldn't. We now know for a fact that all men, and women too, share his passions; but they're not strange anymore. There are no secret lives—no more secrets, no more lives—only "sexuality."

Sex has ceased to be extraordinary, even for ordinary people. Psychologists report that it is fast becoming America's dominant social activity. Everywhere sex is taken casually as legitimate entertainment. "The middle class has the time and energy and money to practice sex as recreation," declares Duane Colglazier, president of Pleasure Chest, Ltd., (and a former Wall Street trader) in an article in the *New York Times*. Although still a young industry, the sex trade has become a multi-billion-dollar business with the characteristics of many conventional industries—a large work force, high-salaried executives, brisk competition, trade publications, board meetings, and sales conventions. Dildoes and vibrators can be charged to Visa or Mastercard accounts, like the more conceptual "phone fantasies." The videotape business has achieved its first major breakthrough by plugging into the sex industry. A Washington-based sex-trade newsletter estimates that the sex business has "the same potential for sales and profits as the food industry. It is a growth industry that cannot go backwards."

Are we getting closer to what Henry Miller dreamingly called the Land of Fuck—a land free from superstition, ritual, idolatry, and fear? "What a man's sex life may be under a new order," he exclaimed, "surpasses my feeble imagination to describe." It really didn't take that much imagination. The "mysterious and unknown, possibly forever unknowable" World of Sex rapidly turned into another Disneyland.

William Masters himself recently pulled the alarm. While studying the behavior of gamblers and drug addicts, it suddenly occurred to him that sex was getting out of hand. It was becoming a prime neurotic habit, another morbid flight into irresponsibility. More than drugs, "sexual addiction" is threatening to turn aggressive professionals into helpless junkies. After two decades of remedial orgasms, crash forms of therapy are being hastily put together to check this crippling hyperactivity.

It may not be an easy task. "The pressure from the culture is very strong *not* to be chaste," asserts Dr. Joyce Brothers. "Nobody wants to hear about your interest in electronics but how many women you have," declares Carl Clay, director of the Black Spectrum Theater, in the same *New York Times* report noted above. "The media projects that sex must always be on your mind. Every record says, Do it, do it . . ."

There's something strangely disquieting in these concerted attempts to convince ourselves that more is better. In 1942, Reich suggested that man is the only biological species to have destroyed its own natural sex functions. He obviously believed that "sex economists," like people's commissars, could help reverse this trend and restore human sexual instinct to its pristine happiness. We're slowly coming to the realization that not only sex, but every single natural function, is now being irremediably destroyed in the human species, including the biological survival of the species itself. Yet for all his courage and inspired madness, Reich unintentionally confirmed Freud's growing disillusion with the civilization. By putting sex even more squarely at the heart of the social process, Reich didn't help inaugurate a new order founded on a "rational sexual policy"; he simply sent sex spinning all the more hopelessly in the empty sky of the culture.

The clinic I discovered wasn't especially concerned with the "right to orgasm." Its patients had none of the anxieties derived from the pressure to perform drilled into the public by well-publicized statistics. These people were in trouble because they performed all too well. Rapists, sadists, pedophiles, frotteurs, voyeurs, and exhibitionists—a whole population of "perverts"—were calling upon these special Sexual Behavior Clinics, hoping to be turned into potential customers for Masters and Johnson.

For five years I followed, step by step, this innovative approach to "sexual deviations," which is faithfully recreated here from actual interviews, tapes, tests, and testimonies. It makes a fascinating document on the way human desires—however undesirable—are now being dealt with, both in the lab and in actual life; it shows the behaviorist's mind at work, alert, resourceful, expedient, impatient with drawn-out therapies and unencumbered by theoretical elaborations, brushing away in one single stroke two thousand years of Western civilization; it finally affords a telescopic vision of the kind of sexuality that is in the offing.

"Is my generation to be the last with bittersweet memories of nearing the threshold of knowledge, of reaching in the dark, of the feel of skin on skin, no consummation, yet a beating of the heart and a flush from the feeling of having transgressed?" Thus sighed a reader to the *New York Times* recently. Yet at the threshold of this century, Paul Cézanne had already summed it all up in one formula: "Everything is about to disappear. You've got to hurry if you want to see things."

Like so many other distinctions—gender, class, ideology —the difference between normality and perversion is becoming blurred (the term "perversion" is avoided today for its moral connotations). When mental patients are let loose in the streets and state prisons are turned over to private enterprise, it becomes difficult to distinguish between crime and business, madness and sanity. When the "whole gamut of sexual practice is presented like a fast-food menu, in newspapers, on television, in schools," the nostalgic reader in the *New York Times* went on, it isn't easy to know what is normal and what is not. All the more reason to see the genders as different species, classes as political essences (terrorism), and ideologies as religions ("evil empires"); all the more reason to deprive mental patients of all their rights and blame a handful of "deviates" for molesting children by the millions. As Claude Lévi-Strauss rightly perceived, the extenuation of differences turns major mythologies into cheap serials. They are no less violent for being emptied of all content.

Sexual deviations, like everything else, have grown democratic. Freud's French master, the celebrated alienist Charcot, used to present his hysterical cases on the stage of the Salpêtrière, ready to perform, in a seductive négligé, for a select audience their most erotic "crises." Today's hysteria affects women and men alike, but no one pays much attention anymore, unless it leads to collective suicide or mass murder. Like Charcot's "great hysterics," the age of the great debauchees and libertines—cynical, satanical, dissolute—is definitely over.

Etymologically, the Latin *deviare* means turning aside from the correct path, departing from the *media via*, the middle way, the established standard, the prescribed course (or intercourse)—diverging from the practice or doctrine that is considered normal among a certain group or society. From the Greek Dionysia to medieval carnivals, however, history offers numerous instances of "perverse" tendencies that found collective expression so threatening to social order that they had to be checked or suppressed altogether. Behind every lonely "deviation" looms a mythical community, which occasionally finds its outlet in philosophical fiction (de Sade), and eventually turns into a "minority culture" (gays, lesbians, etc.).

In the current vocabulary of sexuality, "deviate" is a

euphemism for the once flamboyant, but damning, label of "pervert." (*Pervertere*, to overturn, has actually quite the same meaning as *deviare*.) Perverts have often been perceived as an active and corruptive element, a daring and devastating challenge to social mores. Heliogabalus, the decadent Roman Emperor—Antonin Artaud dubbed him the Anarchist Crowned—waged the Crusade of Sex carrying "a male member instead of cross, lance, or sword." He sought to destroy all value and order, humiliating in himself the principles of authority and reverence to the gods. Gilles de Rais, Joan of Arc's ruthless companion (he was the model for the legendary Bluebeard) exerted his waning feudal prerogatives over the throbbing bodies of his little victims.

Smeared with sperm and bathed in blood, these "sacred monsters" (as Georges Bataille called them) were truly exceptional characters who sought to "overturn" the laws of humanity through a concerted enterprise of demoralization. Aristocrats of vice, like the Marquis de Sade, they were philosophers in the flesh, the embodiment of the demonic forces at work in rationality, forcing life to achieve through their excess and violence the higher state of infamous poetry.

This is, at any rate, how they were viewed by the last gothic visionaries of the modernist imagination. Contemporary "perverts" are neither monsters nor poets. Rapists, says one of their victims, are "some of the most pathetic creatures that walk the earth." Most of them are not, so to speak, full-fledged or professional "deviates," but small-time, occasional sex offenders, decent family people for the most part. They share their mental makeup with their victims. The three rapists who were guests on the popular "Oprah Winfrey Show" along with three rape victims—a strange ritual of self-mortification and collective catharsis —attributed their crimes less to an overwhelming sexual compulsion than to the frustrations of everyday life. "I guess the main thing is self-esteem," flatly declared one of the rapists, who admitted committing his crimes whenever he felt "down, depressed, inadequate, unwanted, unliked." What can be more normal than worrying about one's self-image—and reclaiming it on someone else's back?

The attempt to establish a definitive catalogue of sexual aberrations throughout the nineteenth century testified that "sexuality" was coming to the fore. It was becoming urgent to contain its various expressions. The medical institution quickly substituted its own definitions for ailing cultural and religious codifications. Perversions were (partially) protected from moral or legal condemnation, only to find themselves segregated in a new "perverse constitution."

In his first studies on sexuality, Freud referred often to his positivist elders (Krafft-Ebing, Moebius, Havelock Ellis, Moll, etc.), but he quickly moved beyond mere neurophysiological explanations of "moral monomania" to postulate the existence of a common "sexual drive" running through the whole range of psychic formations. By the same token, it proved impossible to draw a sharp line between variations of "normal sexual conduct" and "pathological symptoms." If, as Freud asserted, perverse tendencies are present in everyone, then perverts, far from being helpless maniacs or hopeless degenerates, may be considered "successful neurotics"—just as Jacques Lacan dubbed parapraxes "successful slips." Perversion is the negative side of neurosis, since it succeeds in implementing the desires that keep lurching at the threshold of inhibited consciousness.

Freud went even further. In his *Three Essays on the The-*

ory of Sexuality (1905), he demonstrated that the poly-morphous perverse constitution is present in the early stages of human development. What this really meant is that the sexuality of the child is essentially open-ended and exploratory, not focused on genitality, and, like libido itself, genderless. To call this free-flowing polymorphous condition "perverse" was an obvious attempt to check the anarchistic tendencies Freud himself had recognized in the human psyche. How can child sexuality be perverse before it can be made to internalize moral and social repression?

The polymorphous hypothesis goes a long way in relo-cating "perversions" at the heart of normality. It suggests that there's no such thing as sexual deviation, only differ-ent states of desire that keep crisscrossing—and occasion-ally colliding with—the changing boundaries of social acceptability. The decision in 1974 by the Psychiatric As-sociation of America to drop homosexuality from their list of "deviations" belatedly confirms the arbitrariness of any sexual discrimination.

It is now possible to free Freudian intuitions from their last moralistic tenets and envisage human sexuality as an unlimited "polysexual" patchwork that resists denomina-tion; if at all, it can be distributed among pragmatic or programmatic categories that owe little, or nothing, to normative considerations: self-sex, soft sex, violent sex, corporate sex, alimentary sex, liquid sex, morbid sex . . . It is this deadpan parody of psychiatric classifications, this utopia instantly realized by "thematically" reshuffling sexual cards and sexual codes that informs the remarkable "Polysexuality" issue of *Semiotext[e]* edited by François Peraldi.

What does it mean to insist on the pluralistic aspect of sexuality? Simply that the notion of "deviance" is a fan-tasy of normality (sexual crime, however, is an altogether different story). Normal sexuality, says Dr. Peraldi, is "the inevitable model against which most psychoanalysts compare polysexuality in order to describe it in terms of deviance." Their reasoning is also circuitous, "perversions" being often used as gradients to define normality! Sexual normality is measured by its degree of proximity or deviation from deviance; at best, it is a statistical fiction.

In *The Hundred Twenty Days of Sodom* (which de Sade disclaims with ambivalent humor as "the most impure tale that has ever been told since our world began") the divine Marquis dismisses in advance any attempt to establish a "science" of sexuality. Isolating and graduating lecherous excesses, he declares, "would perhaps perform one of the most splendid labors which might be undertaken in the study of manners." For this uncanny forerunner of Krafft-Ebing, however, differences are not meant to be cordoned off in circumspect "cases," like animals in a cage; they are called forth to inflame the imagination. "It is up to you," he warns, "to take what you please and leave the rest alone, another reader will do the same, and little by little, everyone will find himself satisfied." Establishing a norm leaves everyone discontented, inhibiting the many, and arresting the rest. Unless, as de Sade cunningly suggests, "the true way of extending one's desires is to attempt to impose checks upon them." Is the norm, after all, an invention of the perverse?

Georges Bataille, the author of *Death and Sensuality*, is probably the last to have addressed this question in earnest. Sexuality, he realized, couldn't survive without sacrificial violence. Being himself a faithless mystic, he was perverse enough to dare our culture to confront the religious roots of its fascination. There may still be something of this transgressive intent in the fascination for the "ultimate sex" which permeates the *Semiotext[e]* volume on "Polysexuality," as if libido freed from inhibition had to find its limit, or its accomplishment, in the death drive.

Sexuality can't be easily rationalized. It has to do with obscure forces that often erupt beyond anyone's control. But violence can be put to use, suspending the crippling effects of rationality. This is the function it assumes in sadomasochism, which is not a gratuitous exercise in private fascism, but a highly ritualistic form of "social therapy." By submitting his slave to a dizzying spiral of violence and eroticism, the master promises him more than pleasure: he strips the slave of the inhibitions that prevent him from taking responsibility for his own existence. Death is not the goal here, but the internal horizon (and occasionally the supreme temptation) of a subjective rebirth.

While neurosis has been explained away ad nauseam, "perversions" curiously remain uncharted territory. There is a reason for this, which Freud was quick to perceive: "Perverts who can obtain satisfaction," he wrote, "do not often have occasion to come for analysis." And why should they? Inhibited individuals come for analysis because of the severe limitations they put on their behavior. They are, so to speak, covert perverts. They express their "aberrant instincts" in twisted ways, turning pleasure into mental torture, or physical discomfort. Neurotics exhibit the riddle of their desires in symptoms that elude their own grasp. They need the talking cure to solve and dissolve these painful "formations."

"Perverts" usually don't need psychiatrists to tell them what they are. They've learned it first hand, experimenting with their own desires, breaking apart and putting together in a different fashion the various pieces of their subjectivity. Masochists are often natural geniuses of psychology, and specialists in their own right. If they come into analysis at all, they resist the psychiatrist's authority, ignoring the mechanism of transference upon which the cure relies. All too often, psychiatrists find themselves hopelessly drawn into a verbal challenge which ridicules the therapy, or forced to adopt a moralizing position which belies—and questions—the reality of their function. What can be more humiliating for a psychiatrist than to be out-played at his own game by a masochist?

For Freud, perverts are uninhibited neurotics. As he saw them, perversions develop when, resisting integration (which Freud values as normality) the various components of the sexual instincts come apart and express themselves directly through definite gestures (exhibitionists), attitudes (voyeurs), practices (masochists), or actions (sadists). The strange formations perverts resort to—fetishes, scenarios, contracts—are just some of the protocols that secure their satisfaction and their sanity without the resort to analysis.

It may be misleading to define perversions by their object. Often, the choice is not spontaneous or "natural"; it is mediated (or dictated) by society. The urge to rape, for instance, may come from a feeling of personal inadequacy, a need for revenge or punishment. Rapists don't feel guilty because they commit a crime, they commit a crime *in order to confirm their guilt*. (Robert Stoller's vision of perversion as a counterrevolutionary force salvaging the oedipal family fits perfectly here.)

Sexual "deviance" may also be a way of challenging society and its "adult" imperatives. I once asked a pedophile if he would love children the same way if the practice were to become legal; he hesitated for a while and answered, "Probably not." For him, pedophilia wasn't just a secret practice, let alone a guilty reaction, it was part of his approach to the world. It meant staying on the margins of legality, like a militant espousing a political cause.

Sexual deviance is a legal sanction as much as a psychological proclivity. No wonder psychiatrists prove unable to define it medically. "Society arrests them," declares one of the doctors interviewed in this book. Another practitioner comments: "All the deviant acts are antisocial in nature. They go against the norm." And a third sums it up: "If you want to live in this society, you have to abide by its laws."

Although sex offenders are the minority, all "deviates" are generally perceived as potential criminals, more frightening than actual muggers and murderers whose motives—need, greed, or passion—everyone can at least understand or identify with. In a world where individual motivations are being explained away before they are even (or ever) experienced, deviates remain tauntingly unscrutable. Like Richard Hambleton's threatening silhouettes painted in dark corners of Manhattan, the shadowy figure of the pervert keeps hovering around the fringes of society, haunting its deepest dreams, the object of an unavowable fascination which episodically erupts into violent hysteria and revulsion.

The current campaign against child molesters is exemplary in this respect. Although what filters down through the press clearly designates families and "trusted adults" as the primary threat to children's welfare, media enquiries always end up with the indictment of individual pedophiles, immediately compounded with rumors—often unfounded—of elaborate pervert "rings."

The current outcry is reminiscent of the kind of outrage Freud met with when he first introduced the notion of child sexuality to the scientific community. Freud recognized that, long before puberty, the child is "capable of mature love, lacking only the ability for reproduction." But the sexual revolution Freud inaugurated relied precisely on the liberation of love, or sex, from reproductive principles. The recognition of children's sexuality went together with the movement of capital, which freed from traditional tutelage and segregated status whomever could assume the enviable role of producer/consumer, regardless of age. Are pedophiles to be held solely responsible for our society's tendency to neutralize all barriers, be they sexual, generational, or social?

For close to a century, we've tracked down children's shifting moods and desires, casting them practically from the womb into the rigid grid of adult sexuality. What if children simply wanted to be left alone, altogether free from the burden of the flesh—spared enforced enlightenment or puritanical obsessions, as well as one-sided lusts?

"We try and stay away from using youngsters, but some of these kids are so beautiful you can't help but use them," an editor declared to the *New York Times*, commenting upon the current invasion of twelve-year-old "pretty babies" fighting their way onto the covers of fashion magazines—with their parents' active support, of course. One child's agent added even more bluntly, "What is most sellable now is a real seductive baby face." So who is seducing whom? Who is using and abusing whom? Should we put the entire adult community, which in so many ways encourages and profits from such impulses, under strict surveillance?

"There's something disturbing here," concluded the *New York Times*. "Is it decadence—Humbert Humbert gone commercial?" It is decadence, indeed. It has become standard practice to erect sexual (in this case youthful) fantasies that sell, while the actual desires raised in children and adults alike are not dealt with openly.

Our society desperately needs monsters to reclaim its own moral virginity. It doesn't hesitate to encourage and exploit sexuality in all its forms—all the more reason to cordon off children in a fantasy world, a sacred kingdom of helplessness and innocence inhabited by good little savages, a private colony unheeded by the ebb and flow of history and the abyss of capitalist decadence in which we are being engulfed, for better or for worse.

We can't reason the issue of pedophilia. We're touching here one of the thresholds of our culture, possibly the very last, where our society has stored away whatever is left of its old values. These fantasies are our last refuge. If they were to fail us, we wouldn't know anymore where, and for whom, to ground our morality.

We live in a society that is curiously ambivalent about its own standards, let alone about its own reality. While claiming that sexuality is repressed, it makes it serve everywhere in the most blatant fashion. The more fundamental the drive, the more pressure there is to use it for other purposes—psychological, cultural, economical, political.

In most societies sexuality is far less formative of the culture than death. Ours brings sexuality to center stage, while death, unrecognized, occupies all the remaining space. Fear of death floats aimlessly everywhere, ready to pounce on anyone, given the chance. Anxiety is not, as Freud assumed, primarily a result of sexual inhibition; on the contrary, sex is obsessively *exhibited* everywhere in order to fill the hole. (Psychoanalysis has simply managed to *displace* our fears.) Like Hegel's slave, who abdicates his freedom to remain alive, we certainly deserve our inferior (neurotic) psychic condition.

In spite of its clinical definition, neurosis is not an illness, it is the paradoxical form of normality. Society maintains the individual on the verge of breakdown, "pushing" its protection in return for a degree of submission.

Michel Foucault's provocative proposition that "modern society is perverse" makes even more sense in this context. It is perverse, he says, "not in spite of its puritanism or as if from a backlash provoked by its hypocrisy; it is in actual fact, and directly perverse." In his *History of Sexuality*

Foucault argued that the proliferation of discourses around sex in the nineteenth century had the effect of multiplying and intensifying disparate sexualities, not curbing them. But modern society is twice perverse since it wraps sexuality tightly around the fragile individual like a mummy in order to shield him from his fears. The fascination with death—"snuffing"—perversely returns to sexuality a dimension it was set up to exorcize.

It has been argued (even in the face of AIDS) that death gives sexuality a chance to regain the sense of purpose and gravity that was lost when it was made to serve every possible consumer impulse. Breaking down the individual's immune system, fear of death, however, ends up leaving him even more vulnerable to the pressure of society. Reclaiming sexuality from social waste would require at this point a new attitude toward life—less frantic, more festive —and a much needed reintegration of death in the culture (beyond the therapeutic anesthesia administered by Elizabeth Kübler-Ross).

Confronting violence and death through sexuality, sadomasochism may be a baroque attempt in that direction. This would explain its growing audience. Such extreme remedy explodes in one movement the boundaries of subjectivity and the stratifications of society.

The masochist "deviates" from the norm because he is *excessively* normal and moral. His alienation from society is, indeed, so acute that he can only hope to repossess himself by transfering to his master alone all his needs for acceptance.

The master is treated as a god, and obeyed unquestioningly, but he is also *totally* accountable for his action. If he were to fail to restrain his own violence, misjudging the physical endurance or the psychic condition of his "bottom," his power would instantly evaporate. This explains why masochists are to be counted by the thousands, but true sadists (as distinct from psychopaths) only by the dozens.

Sadomasochism strives to avoid the dialectics of master and slave—Hegel's con game—which in the "real world" perverts all the energies in dubious confrontations. The purpose of the sadomasochist contract is precisely to make sure that power is never at stake. The bottom doesn't compete with his master; he manages with his help to challenge his own limits. The two configurations overlap, both struggling to achieve separately their own singularity.

Deviates are maximalists of desire in a society which puts sex everywhere except in sexuality. These are people who don't "consume" sex indiscriminately or metaphorically, as nice "normals" do; they take the injunction to experience life in sexual terms literally, asserting through their behavior (and, alternately, their crimes) the purely sexual nature of sexuality.

Paradoxically, though, the more they stake their claims on sex alone (like the author of *My Secret Life*) the more their sexuality "deconstructs" every single aspect of society.

Voyeurs testify to the disappearance of sexual secrecy. Flashers reveal the fallacy that regulates sexual relations. Rapists fulfill paroxysmically society's desire to possess women as objects. Masochists give their bodies to the commodification of desire. Sadists vindicate the random violence exemplified everywhere. Pedophiles betray the fact that children too are "on the market." Frotteurs rub against the fact that sex is replacing human contacts.

Biologists isolate strains of a virus to test the total configuration; concentrating in themselves tendencies otherwise diffuse throughout society, "perverts" strain normality to the limit, by the same token revealing sexuality, and society, for what they are.

Jacques Lacan once wrote that the unconscious posed a

question *with* the hysteric, as one poses a problem *with* a pen. The enigma of hysteria—the tortured, hieroglyphed bodies that medicine couldn't account for organically—challenged psychiatry to come up with another, more devious, or deviant, form of knowledge. Psychoanalysis managed to make these silent signs speak for themselves, or in spite of themselves.

Sexual "deviates" are likewise an enigma, and it is the future of the culture that they are challenging us to decipher through their obsessions. This is the question—and the form of knowledge—that I would like to pose—and expose—*with* this study.

1

Arouse

This training tape is developed for individuals who carry out some type of behavior that could lead to their arrest.

You are seeing this tape because you have this attraction or you carry out a variety of sexual behaviors that are against the law or are uncomfortable for your family or others. Without this arousal pattern—today we will focus mostly on individuals who are involved with children—without this interest in children, without your desire to be involved sexually with them, your life would be a lot simpler—because that desire for children has led to your arrest.

*Now you have to carry out a treatment that will help
you control those urges. If you don't—although there is
a reduction in your interest in children temporarily
after arrest, because of the heat coming from your family, or your employer being aware of your behavior—
after that clears away, your interest comes back and you
are faced with the same problem: having to deal with
these urges that have led to your arrest.*

*There are different ways of approaching this problem.
Today we are going to discuss the treatment method
that we have found to be exceedingly effective at destroying or eliminating your interest in children for sexual reasons . . .*

Dr. Seymour Sachs is speaking on a video monitor at the
Center for Sexual Behavior, in Chicago, a massive building
overlooking the lake. This introductory tape is shown to
incoming patients when they enter the lab for evaluation.
Dr. Sachs is the head of the clinic.

"Could you tell me what all these machines are for?" I
ask Ted Taylor, the lab technician.

"Certainly," he says. "Here we measure sexual
arousal."

"How do you measure that?"

"Well, we use a Barlow Strain Gauge. It's called a penile
transducer. The technique is about ten years old. It consists simply of a rubber band circling the penis. Let me get
one and I'll show you. This is one." He snaps it. "It's a
plastic tube filled with mercury. As you can see, it's made
of two columns, one of mercury and one of rubber. Two
bead wires go into this juncture point and from that point
into a circle. The circle is elastic, naturally, and goes
around the penis. As the elastic band distends, or as
the penis grows larger, it pushes this string gauge farther
apart. I'll show you how it works. It's almost like a thermo-
meter . . . After the patients have been interviewed by the

doctor, they come in and put the gauge around their penis."

"One person at a time?"

"Oh yes, one at a time."

"Is the patient naked?"

"He's semiundressed. His clothes have to be away from the gauge because of the sensitivity of the machine. We ask the subject to place the gauge three-quarters of the way back on the penis. This prevents movement down the shaft and also avoids any problems caused by body hair. We can measure very low, very minute erectile responses by increasing the sensitivity of the machine. If the penis is small, we have different kinds of gauges. The only problem is when the person is obese—the belly may actually sit on the penis.

"The gauge is calibrated using a calibrator cone, which is a graduated cone made of acrylic material. It's done in steps from a low point of 6.5 centimeters in circumference expansion of the gauge to 14 centimeters in circumference, in 5-millimeter expanding steps. We use that cone to calibrate it on a polygraph. As we move it down the cone, we can see that it moves in a linear progression: one millimeter increase in the circumference of the penis is equal to one millimeter upward deflection of the pen on the polygraph."

"Is this kind of measurement pretty widespread?"

"It is useful for night-time work."

"What do you mean by night-time work?"

"Sleep research. It's found that during REM sleep, men have erections. It's called nocturnal penile tumescence. If a man doesn't get erections during REM sleep, he might have an organic problem. It's a diagnostic treatment mostly used in hospitals for sleep disorders and in sex clinics. Only a few clinics use it as we do, monitoring erection response."

"It seems there are no women offenders. Why's that?"

"Well, that's a good point."

"Your population is entirely male, right?"

"Right. That's where the problem seems to lie."

"And there is no program for women."

"No."

"No women are being treated for sexual offenses?"

"We don't get any here, but it definitely exists. It would be naïve to believe that it doesn't. William Masters published a paper which reports on five men who'd been the victims of rape, either by a single woman or by a group of women. In incest programs they have women offenders. But not many. The percentage is so small that people aren't going to invest a lot of money in it."

"So does that mean there aren't any evaluation procedures for women?"

"Oh, those exist. The study of sexual arousal for women is important for the understanding of sexual dysfunctions. The displacement of blood in women can also be measured because it is pooled in one area and changes the body temperature."

"How do you measure that?"

"You take a small thermistor—a temperature-sensitive gauge—and you make up a small clip, like a clothespin, if you like, which you connect to a thermograph. The woman takes the pin and clips it onto one of the lips of her vagina. When the blood rushes in, it changes the temperature and that corresponds to an increase. The other way of measuring it is to take a small tube, 2 to 3 centimeters in length and 1 to 2 centimeters in diameter and section it off. A middle piece blocks the light entirely so that it is received by a photoelectric cell on one side and read on the other side by a light meter. The woman inserts the tube into her vagina so that the wire comes out. The blood rushing in changes the reflectance capabilities of the vaginal walls, so less light is being picked up, and you can measure that . . . But let's get back to the techniques we practice here. There's also plethysmographic evaluation."

"What is that?"

"Plethysmographic evaluation is the measuring of volume changes in the organ. And I tell you, the penis is a good one, because it changes volume enormously; there's lots of blood rushing into it. Anything that happens to the penis you'll see plethysmographically. In order to do that, you have to have the entire organ encased in an airtight or watertight container. When you're using a mercury and rubber strain gauge, you're only measuring the circumference, or the diameter, on one point of the shaft. But there are places in the erection—during the very early stages of the erection cycle—when the two measures diverge. So plethysmographically you'll get an increase, although it decreases circumferentially. It works like this: the blood rushing into the penis forces the organ longitudinally. This movement is first represented as a diameter decrease, very slight obviously (you can't see it with your eyes), although volumetrically—this could be demonstrated; in fact, I did demonstrate it in my thesis—the overall change is registered as a positive increase. If you manage to read my paper—it is a very dry paper—you'll see that I discuss that phenomenon in a lot of depth, with graphs and everything."

"How would you describe this plethysmographic contraption? How is it constructed?"

"Well, it's a very complex instrument. I'll show you one. It's a glass tube . . ."

"How big?"

"The size of a penis, larger actually. It's sealed off at the end with a cuff made of soft, rubberlike material pressed against the body and attached at the back, so that a seal is made with the body around the penis. The person puts a prophylactic on his penis, and when the penis starts to get larger, it creates a certain amount of pressure in this tube, displacing the air. And this air can be measured and represented graphically."

"How do you get a condom on a soft penis?"

"The patient only puts it halfway down the penile shaft. It may take him three or four tries, but usually it stays."

"But the walls of the machine don't really touch the penis."

"No, but if the penis is flaccid, it will fall down and touch the glass tube. That's why patients have a condom on, so that there is no contamination from it."

"Is the plethysmograph less used than the penile transducer?"

"Yes. This machine is a lot more intrusive than the rubber gauge. It bothers the subjects more. They have to put the harness on, introduce their penis into a tube . . . The transducer is portable, which this apparatus is not. The preparation is easier, faster to explain, cheaper to do, and frankly, you get equivalent results."

"And this machine over there with the polygraph paper, what is it for?"

"It's a standard Grass Polygraph machine. Grass is the name of the manufacturer. Grass and Beckman. It's the one preferred by most researchers. It can also be used as a lie detector and for numerous psychophysiological assessments. It can monitor pulse, respiration, sleep EEGs, heart rate, EEG for brain waves, etc. We just use it to score the erections."

"Erection to what?"

"Patients listen to tapes through these headphones. The tapes are short descriptions of sexual scenes with kids. It could be something like: 'You're with a young girl. You're taking her pants off. You're making her touch your penis.' "

"I see."

"Or something like: 'You're holding a little boy from behind. You're pushing your dick in and out of his asshole.' "

"I see."

"Or: 'You're following a ten-year-old girl onto the train. It's packed. You're moving right up behind her and you start feeling her ass and tits. She's frightened.' "

"Uh . . . this gauge around the penis, is it connected to the needle?"

"When I stretch the gauge, the little needle goes up, as you can see."

"Yes, it goes up."

"So we can measure, over time, arousal to the stimuli. There are sixteen of these tapes, all of different kinds. One kind is mutual consent between a child and an adult—the child is not protesting. Another tape is verbal coercion—just verbal—urging the child to have sex. The tape might go: 'You're telling the child he better take his pants off or he'll get hurt.' It's a narrative description in the third person. Actually it's in the *second* person: *You're* raping this, *you're* raping that."

"I find it interesting that you make this distinction, because in linguistics the second person implies the presence of the first, while the third, 'he's raping,' is purely referential. So when you address me with the second person pronoun, saying, '*You* are raping' . . . actually, *you* and *I* become reversible . . ."

"Another tape involves physical coercion—actually holding the child down: 'You're holding a pretty girl down as you eat her. You can feel your dick getting hard.' "

"Actually . . ."

"What?"

"Nothing. I'm sorry."

"Another tape involves sadistic coercion, tying the child down, hitting him hard, making him bleed: 'You've stuck a water hose up a girl's cunt and you're turning on the water full force. She's begging you to stop.' "

"My God!"

"Another tape separates the sex from the assault: 'You're hitting a young boy in the face. He's crying out in pain.' Just assault, just hitting the child, with no sexual component. We want to see if they get aroused only to the aggressive component and not the sexual. Another tape is an incest tape, in which they're having sex with their daughter—or son, in the case of homosexuals: 'Your son is curled up beside you in bed. You're rubbing his small penis. He's getting an erection.' Or again: 'You're unbuttoning your daughter's blouse. You're feeling her small tits. She likes it.'

"We've found that about 30 percent of our patients, on the average, have engaged in behavior with young boys. However, most of these men also have adult arousal to women. They are not homosexuals with adults, but they also like young boys. We find that very few of our patients are actually fully homosexual. They're not involved exclusively with young boys and, contrary to most of the definitions in diagnostic manuals, they're not exclusively involved in one arousal pattern or one acting out. They are also involved in other, normative, sexual patterns, and sometimes multiple paraphilias—sexual deviations—as well."

"So people who focus on only one paraphilia are the exception."

"Yes. They're exceptions to the norm, which is why it's going unreported, or underreported. This is often said of other issues, too, of people who commit murders: 'I worked next to him for twelve years and he seems such a nice man.' Well, he *was*, from nine to five. He was a good worker—and also at nine o'clock at night he'd go out and shoot people who had long blond hair, or black hair."

"People always imagine deviates as loners or sociopaths . . ."

"They're human beings. They all belong to one race, the
human race. It affects people straight across the board,
across the socioeconomic status, across training; it doesn't
stop at a degree or a bank account. Nor does cancer, or
high blood pressure, or any disorder. That's our basic premise."

"So what you're saying is that anyone can be a deviate."

"Yes."

"Do you mind addressing me in the second person as if I
were one of your patients?"

"Not at all. One of the things we do here at the clinic is
try to get some kind of objective measure of what you are
aroused to. Now, you're going to come into this room here,
and sit in this chair. You're going to put this string-gauge
on, three-quarters of the way up your penis. The way you
put the gauge on is as follows: you just spread it out with
the fingers of one hand, and put it on the penis—just kind
of place it on."

"This way?"

"Try not to roll it on, because the gauge will twist.
Okay? Also make sure your clothing is out of the way so
that there's no impinging from your body movements.
Now, you'll do this totally in your own privacy. I'll leave
the room when you do it. Okay?"

"Okay."

"At this point we make an initial measurement, which
we call a baseline measurement, so that you will always
come back to that zero point. We check to make sure that
indeed you're flaccid, that you have zero percent erection,
in our terminology. Now I'll got out there and talk to you
over the intercom . . .

"Are you ready?"

"Zero percent."

"Let me tell you how we're going to proceed. You'll be listening to sixteen two-minute-long tapes. Before each tape, I'll give you one of two instructions. I'll say either 'arouse,' or 'suppress.' If I say 'arouse,' it means that I want you to listen to the tape and imagine yourself as being a part of the scene that is being described. And if you should get an erection, just let it happen. If I say 'suppress' before the tape, once again imagine yourself in that scene, but if you feel yourself getting an erection, try to suppress it. Try to block it out with your mind. But at no time should you touch the gauge at all. And you should try to sit fairly still, because if you move, the gauge may also move, and the machine may think that you have an erection when you don't. So it is to your advantage to sit as still as you can."

The technician goes out of the room and closes the metal door behind him. I put the apparatus on.

"Let's start the tape now."

My partner and I are at a drive-in movie. She has unbuttoned her blouse for me. I'm feeling her tits . . .

My head is lying on the hairy chest of a strong, muscular guy . . .

I'm lying across a bed as a woman spanks me across the ass with her belt . . .

I scream out as a woman bites into my arms and scratches near my balls with her long, sharp fingernails . . .

While I'm working in a customer's house, I pause by a teenage girl's bedroom. I watch her as she looks at herself nude in the mirror . . .

I'm on a subway train, rubbing an attractive woman's breasts. She's moving in closer to me and smiling . . .

"What should I do?"
"What did you say?"

I'm rubbing my dick through the silk panties I have on. I've got an erection . . .

Through a window, late at night, I'm watching a twenty-year-old woman squirming around on her bed, touching her breasts and genitals. She doesn't know I'm watching her . . .

It's the afternoon. Two young girls on a motorscooter are looking at my penis. They are really excited . . .

My partner and I have been fucking all over the room. Now we are standing up. I've got my arms around her ass, fucking her in front of the mirror . . .

"Should I suppress or arouse?"
"Just let it happen."

I'm in an attractive woman. She's very tight and wet. She's enjoying it quite a lot . . .

A huge man is holding me down against the ground. I can't even struggle. He's about to stick his dick in my ass . . .

My six-year-old daughter is sitting on my lap, playing with the hair on my chest. She's teasing me and I feel myself getting aroused . . .

I'm forcing a well-stacked girl to hold still as I push my dick into her. She cries out as I rape her . . .

I've put on a bra and I'm looking at myself in the mirror . . .

I've cut a woman's breasts off with my knife and I'm squeezing the blood out of them . . .

"Ugh . . ."

I'm coming out of the shower, drying myself off. A ten-year-old girl walks in, sees me, and we're both surprised. I want to stay there and let her look . . .

I've knocked the woman unconscious. I'm about to cut her open, starting at her cunt up to her tits. I'm going to take out her insides.

"Please . . ."

I'm in a subway. Everyone is pushing. I'm facing a woman. I let my hand touch her vagina while she looks right at me . . .

I'm fucking my daughter. I feel her smooth little body beneath mine . . .

"Now, after each tape there are three things that I'm going to say. The first thing will be 'pleasure.' I'll ask you how pleasurable the tape was, and you give me a rating on a scale of minus 3 to plus 3. If you liked the tape a lot, you would say 'plus 3,' and if you hated it, you would say 'minus 3.' If you liked it a little, you might say 'plus 1' or 'plus 2.' If you didn't like it a little, 'minus 1' or 'minus 2.' 'Zero' would mean that you neither liked nor disliked it. Ready?"

"Uh huh."

I'm lying beside a movie star, playing with her titties. My hands are reaching inside her wet pussy . . .

I'm pulling an eight-year-old girl on top of me. She feels small and soft and warm . . .

I'm surrounded by angry women with knives. They're going to cut me again and again . . .

"You call that 'pleasure'?"

"Got it? Then I'll say, 'Arousal: zero to 100 percent.' What that means is: How arousing was the tape in your mind? If it was just a little bit arousing, you might say '10 percent.' A lot would be 80 or 90 percent. The third thing I'm going to ask you is: How much erection do you think you have? Zero to 100 percent.

"If your penis is just sitting there, just say 'zero.' The lights will be dark and you will not be able to touch your penis, so your estimation might not be very good. You might have a slight erection and not realize it. If you have an erection, I might try to get your mind off the tapes. I might say, 'Count backwards by sevens.' Or I might say, 'Name as many presidents of the United States as you can think of.' Or simply, 'Name streets.' Just to get your mind off the tapes. And this is an effective procedure."

"Is that part of 'suppress'?"

"No. If you get an erection, the next tape can't start until the erection is down. And if I just let you sit there, you might fantasize."

"What's wrong with fantasizing?"

"A lot of fantasy consists of rebel behavior. So in order to block that, I will ask you to do a very monotonous task."

"Hoover, Nixon, Roosevelt, Johnson, Carter, Reagan . . ."

"Right. To prevent you from thinking about the tape. And it generally works. I might say, 'Recite the alphabet backwards,' which is a difficult task. You do the verbal task and I listen over the intercom."

"When do you actually say 'suppress'?"

"If we tell you to suppress and you still get a lot of erection, it indicates to us that you don't have the ability to control it when you want to."

"Why should I want to?"

"Why should you want to? Let's say you are with a kid but you know that if you have sex with that kid, you'll be arrested. If you can control it, you might be more able to stay away from trouble . . . Then you get another run with slides."

"Still using the penile transducer?"

"No. We use a pupillometer."

"What's that for?"

"It measures the dilatation of the pupils in relation to the presentation of stimulus, a mechanism used by many ophthalmologists. It projects infrared onto the eye. There's a television camera which focuses on the pupil. The pupil is outlined and calibrated onto a thing called an eye-view monitor, which measures the size of the pupil. The stimulus comes on, it's presented, and we measure your dilatation and constriction."

"Do you use the polygraph here as well?"

"Yes. The polygraph reproduction of pupillary response is given in terms of what is known technically as a cumulative integrator. What that does is take a signal input from the pupillometer and, in plain language, it just averages it. It gives you a count either as peaks or as so many reactions per second, depending on how you're using the integrator."

Dr. Sachs, the clinic's director, enters behind us, hands in his white jacket.

"This study," he explains, "evolved out of some experimental movies with measurement of pupil size. If this is the eye, and here the pupil looking down, we spray infrared light across the eye and the camera picks up the amount of light on the diameter of the pupil. It records scans continuously, sixty times a second. Now what we do is present various stimuli, various types of sexual activity, in a number of categories: black-and-white pictures of nude boys and girls, a naked girl on a bed, for example, legs wide apart, showing genitalia, a boy standing behind a chair, penis erect; adolescents: a young man taking his pants down, a young woman naked, kneeling on a bed;

adult males or females: a close-up of a man's torso and genitals, a naked woman touching her breast and vagina; four scenes depicting someone being exhibited to: a girl opening the door with an expression of surprise; four scenes dealing with frottage: a male hand on a woman's tight jeans; four sadistic-type scenes of someone tied up: a naked woman with both head and heavy breasts tightly bound; and four neutral scenes. You watch these slides for seven seconds at a time."

"What do you mean by neutral scenes?"

"That's the result of an investigation I did some time ago on how to alter arousal patterns. I was using a switching process, going from deviant to nondeviant. I wanted to see if you could generate a general arousal where it didn't exist before. I looked for something that could be easily visualized, that the person could imagine and see, and yet had no sexual value at all. I selected something from around the area—I was in Mississippi at the time—something that no one could possibly be aroused to."

"What was that?"

"A magnolia tree."

"A magnolia tree? Did you choose a tree because it recalls an erection?"

"Does it? Uh . . . well, it could be deflowered, but that's not the point." He takes out a file. "Look right here at this graph. It's a single-case experimental design—that means that the patient is used as his own control. Fl is a multiple baseline of cross-behaviors. You can see that the individual masturbating to this particular stimulus got it up to 31 percent of an erection."

"You mean that the tree was actually eroticized?"

"Yeah."

"Does it prove that you can get people aroused to anything?"

"Well, the person wasn't aroused to trees before."

"Can it be that magnolia trees are particularly sugges-
tive to human stimulation?"

"It could have been any other tree."

"Did you do anything special to make it more titillat-
ing?"

"I took pictures and I made audiotape descriptions of
someone touching, feeling the magnolia tree. Here on this
graph you can see the individual's masturbatory latency to
ejaculation, in minutes, and over there to the deviant fantasy."

"Was your patient more turned on to trees than to his
own deviant fantasies?"

"No. You wouldn't expect that at all."

"Did he remain aroused to trees?"

"No, he didn't. As you can see on this graph, he was just
able to 'get up' for a little while. It's a touchy testing to
pursue. I did this study in 1969, a long time ago. Now it
would be very difficult to develop arousal patterns where
they didn't exist before in a nonfunctional area, because
of the ethical issue."

"It's not ethical to get people turned on to trees?"

"No."

"What about animals? Have you ever treated cases of
bestiality?"

"Yes. We have treated bestiality, but I've never come
across a person who was turned on to trees."

"Where do you get your slides from?"

"We make them ourselves."

"You actually stage them?"

"Oh, no. The content is taken from magazines, pornography magazines. You can buy them anywhere. But we
mount the pictures ourselves and we take care of any
sculpting that has to be done in terms of light intensity.
Actually we found that this procedure involved very complicated technical problems. First of all, in order to get a

gestalt from a figure, you must have a contrast to it. Take the image of a young boy sitting naked on a bed. If the contrast is very stark, the background will be essentially white and his body silhouetted dark. When the eye looks over to the boy, you can imagine that the pupil will dilate some with respect to the background. So, in order to control this contrast, you can make both the background and the boy gray. You'll still be able to distinguish between them, but the difference won't be that great."

"You try to eliminate extraneous elements in order to isolate the erotic reaction."

"That's it. Now, when you present stimuli on the screen, the lighting of the stimulus itself produces changes in the pupil. Recently we've taken the slide and made a second slide out of it that's out of focus. The pupil adjusts to this blur and establishes a baseline in terms of pupil size. So, by the time the clear slide comes on, the eye has been looking at seven seconds of blur. We're adding a computer program that takes in all this data, analyzes it, averages it from second to second and plots this data, minus the blur. The difference in pupil size is the arousal to the content of the clear picture.

"The computer scores the pupil size thirty times a second. It measures seven seconds per slide. That's 210 data points per slide. And we have forty slides. We used to hand-score the data, and it was a killer. You're measuring such small changes, and scoring such an astronomical number of data points. Without the computer, we could never have done the pupillometry study.

"And it was very problematic; it took us a year to program it right. Besides, we only used data points for seconds four through seven—that's the important data. It all takes three hours, including one hour set-up time and a one-hour run with the patient. We split up two groups: those exclusively attracted to boys, and those exclusively attracted to girls. Out of the twenty-five men we saw, we classified twenty-five out of twenty-five correctly, using the pupils.

"And the pupillometer will do something else. It will throw a light in and bounce it off the cornea. So, if you're looking right here, it will pluck this coordinate. If you look right there, it will pluck that other coordinate. Knowing that these are the edges of the slides, we'll be able to tell, for any second, exactly where you are looking. This machine will keep track of it.

"We'll divide each picture into sixty-four quadrants—the computer does it for us—and we'll have the machine tabulate how much of the total time you have been looking at the figure and how much at the genitals.

"What I've just described is an intraslide problem, but we also have an interslide problem. You have to make sure that the intensity is the same from slide to slide . . ."

"How do you manage to keep the pupil in the same position for so long?"

"The pupillometer comes with a headrest, which is actually a frame containing the head. We added a 'bite board.' This is a metal plate coated with the dental material that's used for impressions. It's very malleable once it's heated. You bite into it and the material is allowed to harden. In that way we have an exact duplicate of your bite. So when you take a rest you can leave the headrest, and when you come back you'll be in the same exact position as you were before. The bite board will hold your head immobile. The eyes will be able to track, but the motion will always be constant. In other words, your peripheral vision will be x amount, but it'll always be that fixed amount."

"And I'm supposed to get aroused in that position?"

"It won't be erection response, it'll be pupillary dilatation, which we think is correlated with an arousal reaction."

"Clenching your teeth on a bite board isn't exactly what I would call a turn-on . . . Have you ever tried to correlate erection response with eye dilatation?"

"We haven't up to this point. We'll do that in the future. We will be using our minicomputer once we have a program that's refined and sophisticated enough to pick up all the data points. Right now, we don't want to complicate the procedure more than we have to."

"What's the purpose of all these measurements?"

"To get information. We get some from a pencil-and-paper test that's common to the analytical school and to most other schools of psychotherapy. The patient is asked to sit down and read each card quickly. It is a subjective report in everyday language, usually two or three sentences long, describing the whole gamut of sexual interaction. The cards were developed a few years ago by psychologists, with some patient input.

"We get three statements: mental arousal, physical reaction, and pleasure, which is an overall reaction. But it's a self-report mechanism and it depends entirely on the patients' ability to fill it out honestly. So what do you do when the self-report is totally unreliable? We make our own measurements. That's the impact of our physio-assessment.

"One of the major findings in this field is that there is a great deal of denial that goes on, a lot of cognitive distortion. It's fairly common that someone will come in and say, 'I don't know why I'm here. I just came to satisfy my wife, certainly not because I'm a child molester. I'm not aroused to children. There was this one incident, I was drunk, I didn't know what I was doing.' Put them in a lab situation, and you get 80 percent erection in response to the cue . . . They also lie a lot in the self-report measures. They attempt to conceal from the technology. They think it's to their advantage."

"Aren't they coming in voluntarily for help?"

"They are here for help, but not always of their own volition. Some of the people I see are pressured by their families, or by their wives. Some have been arrested but the charges were dropped, and they fear getting arrested again. Most of them have had experiences with the courts. Occasionally the police or the courts will pressure them into it, so I get a variety of sources. We put ads in the newspaper. We have public service announcements on radio about the existence of a program for child molesters.

"It's still a voluntary clinic. If they want to walk out, they can. We can't hold anyone here. But they're not all self-motivated. And that's why the subjective report procedures are poor. The laboratory tests help."

"Do you confront them with the results?"

"If they have a lot of arousal in the lab and we show them the measures, sometimes they confess. Most people become quiet, then accept the judgement. A few become very angry and deny the facts, but they're overwhelmed with the results.

"I had a patient who showed an unusual amount of denial. Whenever he came to the 'female mutual'—which means that the woman is agreeable, that there is no coercion on his part—he always claimed that his arousal was very high. But we knew that he played with the gauges, tapping or pulling on them, maybe even masturbating in the dark. We couldn't tell for sure. The only way would be to have a camera in there, but we don't. We can only tell from experience. After you've seen hundreds of records, you know what masturbation looks like. Most of the time, when a patient in the lab responds to a stimulus, there is a slow rise on the polygraph, a fairly fluid line. It's quite rare that you get the kind of phenomenon this patient showed, a jagged line jumping up to the maximum. While he was doing it, I asked him if he had just touched the gauge, or if he had moved. Usually that cools them down a little bit. But no, he totally denied it. He wanted to show us that, yeah, I do get very much aroused by normal stimuli.

"Actually we did a study to investigate just how much patients hide at the beginning. Out of ninety people that were confronted with their lab results, 55 percent told us of new arousal patterns that they hadn't told us about before. Almost all admitted to more paraphilias. Once confronted with the truth, they couldn't get out of it, so they admitted it."

"Can it be that they weren't aware of it?".

"It's no unconscious thing. They are always aware of it. The validity of our study is measured by the individual confirming the findings: 'Yes, I do have this arousal that I didn't tell you about.' They all knew it, they just decided at that point to be honest with us."

"Is there a curve of progressive confidence?"

"Well, I don't know if you'd call that 'progressive confidence.' As time goes on, they always tell you more. You've got to understand, we will have seen them for nine months of treatment and then followed them for twelve months after that, so we've had a tremendous amount of contact with them. The more we are able to help them, the more they reveal. Of course, the more they reveal, the more we're able to help them control their behavior."

"Do you think they want their behavior to be controlled?"

"By and large, sex offenders don't want to give up their arousal. They see it as bad, but it's quite enjoyable as well. And it's only after they see some success in being able to give some of that up that they feel more confident about being more honest with you.

"It's a confidential relationship that we have. They tell me all about the violence they've been involved with, the kids they've molested, and they see that I don't react. I mean, I react in the sense that I help them gain control over their urges, but I'm not turning their names over, or telling their family. They see that none of it goes out of this room. They already know they can tell us about deviant behaviors and not get arrested. By law, we are not allowed to testify against them, even if we are subpoenaed. They know that the information they give us cannot be released without their signature.

"Still, some people don't believe it and distrust us, so I'm sure some trickery goes on. If some individuals want to trick us, if they sit there purposely controlling themselves —and if they're good at it—there is really nothing we can do about it. If it happens, it happens. There is no way of knowing. They could practice thinking about something else while listening to the tapes, or whistle 'Yankee Doodle Dandy,' but most people don't experience this as a fun house. You just don't know what's going to happen.

"Some studies have shown that it's hard for normal men to control arousal if they are watching a pornographic movie, but it's still unclear as to how much they can do that. They could even hold the tape away from their ears —we can't watch what they're doing in there. I'll ask them to evaluate the slides, but they could just close their eyes and not look. Periodically I will ask them, 'What was the last slide you saw?' And if they don't know, I'll just start their run all over again. It is possible for them to cheat with the slides. I'm sure it's happened, and they end up with no arousal in the lab. But much less than if they knew the cops could just walk in and grab their chart whenever they wanted to.

"Some of the motivation for cheating is reduced by giving the patients a number when they come in. Their name is kept secret. Everything is confidential, and we try to stress that as much as we can. That's part of why we don't have a video camera in the room. It would create an atmosphere of distrust. We just can't do that. We have to take the risk of doing it another way."

"Do you double-check in specific cases? Do you have access to police records?"

"No, no, no. Sometimes you'll have a report from another psychiatrist, psychologist, social worker, mental health worker. And sometimes a court report. You get a good idea from what has happened to the patient. If he's been arrested, then on what charge? We've got histories under our certificate of confidentiality, which protects the patient. And then we ask a second person in their environment who knows them pretty well, mostly wives, sometimes relatives. But these results are not used as the diagnosis, simply as an aid in diagnosing. The reason we do the study, and the whole point of finding out the arousal, is to indicate areas of treatment. We tell them what the results are and what we can offer. The decision is left up to the patients."

"And they usually cooperate?"

"I don't believe it's too helpful to explore the cooperation issue with the treatment. I've seen a lot of people who I thought would be good candidates and they didn't turn out to do the therapy. I've seen some terrible candidates who responded quite well to the therapy. So I don't try and determine beforehand whether a person is a good candidate or a bad candidate. And, quite frankly, that hasn't been a problem. It's very easy to tell who's not going to respond. It's the resistant personality, individuals who don't really consider it a big deal to have raped thirty women. Those individuals don't want to do the therapy, and they don't do it.

"I had a candidate not respond . . . Well, it's hard to say 'respond.' Who responds? Who doesn't? Anyway, I did some baselines on him—his baseline latency to ejaculation—

and how erotic various stimuli were before he actually started the therapy. Then he only went seven sessions and I couldn't get him to do any more. He'd rather go to jail!'' Dr. Sachs laughs. "This fellow is an incest case. He's got several daughters and he's been involved with every one of them. He said he's no longer aroused to his fantasies, but I'm not really satisfied with that. That's one case.

"I had another candidate that it has not worked with, either. I don't know why. He happens to be attracted to cutting long-haired boys' hair. When he depicts the boy, he really goes into details, details upon details, until you drown in them. He has tremendous obsessions. He cuts the boy's hair, and he acts as if he is the boy himself. That's what is called a 'borderline' case. It's an individual who's not actively psychotic, but whose personality makeup is severely deteriorated. His arousal is coming down, but I've done him a tremendous number of hours, ten times the treatment anyone else has had . . ."

"What types of 'candidates' are there?"

"Voyeurs, transvestites, fetishists, frotteurs, incest cases, rapists, sadomasochists. The Center for Sexual Behavior functions as a research operation in which we investigate the various types of sexual deviation, primarily child molesters and rapists."

"Why those primarily?"

"That seems to be where the action is. Voyeurs and exhibitionists are what we call 'nuisance behavior.' They are not dangerous, unless they escalate. I've seen people who started their sexual career as voyeurs, first looking at windows and getting closer and closer, until they finally entered the woman's bedroom. It could actually lead to rape. But most of the pressure is to deal with rapists and pedophiles simply because nobody really knows what to do with them. It's a fairly new field, although there's been some research going on for the last twenty years. Our purpose is to find out what their arousal patterns are."

"You call them 'deviates.' Is there the idea that they should be cured?"

"No. Society arrests them. You're arrested if you window-peep in this city. If you get caught, you'll go to jail, even if it's for a short time. All the deviant acts, of course, are antisocial in nature and certainly involve a certain amount of psychopathy."

"You mean violence?"

"I mean going against the norm. I guess it comes down to any sexual act that gets you in trouble with the law."

"Do you follow a penal definition of deviance, rather than a psychological one?"

"Quite frankly, I don't think that's relevant to what I'm talking about."

"Sorry. I thought 'antisocial' wasn't a psychiatric criterion."

"I only fall back on giving you information about child molesters because that's the group I get federal funding to study. I can't talk about things that I'm not funded for."

"Do you ever treat sadists?"

"Sadists are rare birds. You don't see many of those. I don't think anybody does. They are very good at not being caught, and if they are, the legal system interferes and judiciously says: this person is dangerous and needs to be incarcerated. They are not remanded to psychiatric care. Why bother with therapy if they're not going to get out of jail? They are complete sociopaths who rape or who brutalize a child and have absolutely no compunction about it whatsoever. No remorse. The only emotional response would be if they were caught. That would be the inconvenience of it."

"Psychoanalysts say that offenders like being caught."

"I don't believe so. True sociopaths *don't* want to be caught. They're *very* upset by that. One guy who was a murderer and a rapist sat there and said: 'I murdered three prostitutes. I murdered them because they were prostitutes and no one cares. That's the premise I went on, that's the premise I understood to be true. Now society is telling me that it's not true. I find that highly inconvenient.'

"He was a patient at a clinic in Florida. And he did quite well. Later when I met him he told me: 'I'm very upset with myself. You may be upset with this for *your* reasons —and quite frankly I don't care what they are, I don't care what your morality is, or whether you think this is right or wrong. I'm concerned with this because it affects my life. And what's most distressing to me is that *this is something that I can't control*. It's a flaw in my personality, the urge to rape. This is dangerous *to me*, and yet I can't stop myself from doing it. Otherwise I very much can control my life. I'm a very successful businessman. And *nothing—nothing*—should inhibit me from doing well with my life.' "

"He didn't go to jail?"

"He had very good lawyers. And the fact was, they were prostitutes."

"And no one cared."

"And no one cares."

"Do you consider your patients not responsible for what they've done?"

"Not at all. I hold any adult responsible for their actions, unless they are psychotic. These patients are not psychotic. We find that cognitive distortions are used, obviously, to ward off feelings of guilt or to continue with their sexual life—and this is their sexual life."

"But the definition of a child molester varies from state to state, not to mention country to country."

"Yes, it varies tremendously, but I believe it's wrong for individuals to commit crimes against people without their consent. Uh . . . and I don't think children can give consent."

"I happen to have met children, thirteen-year-olds, who

actively sought out a relationship with an adult. They just loved older men, their experience, their double chins . . ."

"The child may say yes, but does he really understand the implications? Legally, the child can't consent. The criteria that I go by is that the patient says he is molesting children less than thirteen years old, and that there's five years difference between the child and he."

"What if the legislation were to change?"

"There are still people who are dissatisfied with their behavior, no matter what the law is. Yes, it may be some time in the future that the law will be changed. That may happen. But I can't think over a day ahead."

2
Tease

"If you're doing a treatment that you want to validate, you jolly well better know what's going on in the heads of the patients. That's one of my concerns about analysis and why I've chosen instead to investigate sexual arousal patterns.

"We know that there are a variety of means to measure the sexual arousal physiologically, but the one with the greatest validity is to directly record the erection response. Recording sexual arousal, that's highly erotic, uh . . . I mean, objective.

"There are exceptions to this. Some males have full erection and are not sexually excited. That's called priapism, from Priapus, the phallic god."

"They can't get it down."

"Right. It's a pathological condition in males. They get erections which they do not want to have, and which sustain themselves over time. But that's a malfunction.

"Quantification of erection response, that's the name of the game. If you are interested in language and its interaction with sex—that's what you're studying, right?—this is the only way I know we can quantify the mind. How do you know what someone is thinking? You can never really look inside—except in the sexual area, if you assume that erections equal thought.

"You can do that most easily in individuals who have rather idiosyncratic sexual arousal, such as sexual deviancy. It's easier, because you can separate out specific items that are most erotic. First of all, you take the parts that aren't exciting and you ditch them. You don't expand on those sections, you destroy them. You can actually use physiologic means to pry and tease apart what is erotic to people.

"Here's an actual case, showing a fellow who happened to say that he was a transsexual. Well, he didn't *say* that, he said that he was excited at the thought of being transformed from a male into a female. Being transformed against his will. The sinister, sadistic nature of the person doing the transformation: that was, he said, highly erotic to him.

"Once put on tape, however, the description of the transformation, just the way he liked it, failed to generate any erection response. We prepared a second tape, a second presentation, in which we described the transformation again. You can see by his erection response that the elements *he* had identified as so highly erotic—the words about the sinister nature of the transformation—weren't erotic at all; it was instead, if you pardon my words, 'having tits and nipples.' Having a woman's body, having feminine organs, *that* was highly erotic to him. So from these erection responses, you can start to tease out what is actually erotic about the words.

"Here's a second case which is also highly individualized. It is a single-case design study of a fellow who said that he was turned on by sandals—women's sandals. On tape number 1, which is two minutes in duration, I described a sandal just the way he said it turned him on. I happened to mention that it was a woman's foot, but I didn't go into a description of the woman at all. It generated a little arousal. Not much, less than 20 percent. I figured that if it wasn't the sandal that was erotic to him, then it had to be something around it. So in tape number 2, I decided to describe a woman's foot instead. Not the woman, just the foot. Here's the graph for that description. See? It generates 80 percent of an erection. Now to make certain that it is indeed the woman's foot and not the sandal that is erotic, I described the sandal again. Once again, very little arousal. Then I knew not only that the sandal failed to generate erection responses, but failed *twice*.

"I listened again to that second experience, which generated so much arousal. I found that I described a woman who is quite responsive. She likes to have her foot felt. So what did I do? I teased out this dotted line right here on the graph—the description of the guy feeling her foot. You can see the high arousal that he gets to the new description of the woman's foot, feeling the foot, and her really enjoying it. So it's a matter of teasing out which elements of his words, which aspects of his concepts, are the real turn-on.

"Then I changed one variable, the responsiveness of the woman. I described the foot of an unresponsive girl. I had him feeling the foot, the same kind of foot, but there was no mention of her enjoying it, or turning her foot in his hands. See what it does: it depresses his arousal. Then I changed that variable again. I put back in the woman's responsiveness, and of course once again I obtained the arousal. It's a way of determining what is erotic to people."

"Once you've defined the erotic zones in language, what do you do with the results?"

"That's exactly what we're talking about: the 'erotic zone.' Well, it depends on what you want to do. If you're dealing with a person whose sexual deviancy gets him arrested and gives him all sorts of grief, then you would eliminate that arousal."

"You eradicate that zone in the language?"

"Uh huh. That's right."

"And by erasing it in the language, you expect to erase it in the behavior?"

"Oh, absolutely. Absolutely."

"Isn't there quite a difference between the two? Language is a representation . . ."

"I realize, yes, there's a difference between behavior and language, behavior and thought. I'm aware of that. But we'll leave that aside for the time being. I think the part that would interest you most is how we destroy the erotic zone. Let me just run an idea by you. This is changing gears, but I'd like to step back a little ways.

"You're familiar now with pupillometer measures. The premise is that different material generates different types of pupillary responses. Pupil size has something to do with the content of whatever you're looking at, whatever you're thinking, or thought processes. Things that you're not aroused to won't dilate your pupils."

"Pupils have erections too?"

"Oh, no. Pupil size measures arousability, that's what it measures. By arousability I don't mean 'erection,' I mean 'interest, attention to.' As I'm now looking at the impact of the various visual stimuli I am presenting, however, I

run into a problem. It has to do with the physical characteristics of the eye. Eyes are used for seeing images. So how
in the dickens do you use that same system to indicate
more than just a response to light—something which is
the mind controlling the eyes? This is some sort of philosophical question.

"It's too hard to work with slides. I want to get away
from that kind of complexity, to something simple where
I can either prove or disprove. We find that tapes are much
more effective in discriminating between deviant and nondeviant arousal. If you get aroused to slides, you may get
aroused to *all* the slides. But if you listen to the tapes, you
tend to be aroused only to those tapes that are related to
your fantasy. If you get aroused, for instance, to tapes with
sex that's not violent, when the violent tapes come on,
you don't get aroused at all. However, with the slides, you
might get aroused to the image of a woman being tied
down. You might not be aroused to the sight of the ropes,
but to the sight of naked breasts."

"Washington, Adams, Jefferson, Madison, Monroe, Jack-
son, Harrison . . ."

"Right!" Dr. Sachs laughs. "That's how you suppress
arousal . . . So at one point we replaced the pictures with
drawings. Line drawings. Not very attractive. But at least
we didn't have to kill ourselves trying to achieve consis-
tency in the amount of light coming from each of the
slides. But it didn't help that much. The pupillometer probably would work better with the verbal than the visual."

"Have you tried to measure the pupil's reaction to verbal
stimuli?"

"It's a very difficult thing to do. There is such a thing as
memory load in processing. A person was given several
numbers to add up or multiply. The general observation
was that as people were remembering the numbers, their
pupils would begin to dilate and, all of a sudden, when

they would give the answer, the pupils would constrict. Unloading would occur."

"That's yet another kind of variable. Can you separate it from the mind's reaction to verbal sexual fantasies?"

"I don't know how fantasy works in terms of the mind. Is fantasy something that just happens out of the blue, or is it something that you think about and elaborate on as you imagine more and more of it?

"What I'm interested in now is the possibility of investigating specific words or small phrases and their ability, in a constant light source, to generate varying amounts of pupillary response."

"From words?"

"From words."

"Pronounced or written?"

"Pronounced. If they're written, then you have to read them. You're back to the physics of the eye again. Ultimately, what I'm interested in, the bottom line, is looking at the arousal quality of aggressive sexual words. Because I see violent people. I would like to see if there is a relationship between their violent attitudes and their response to various words."

"I noticed, for example, that you use the word 'destroy' very often."

"Uh huh . . . They use words like 'slut' and 'bitch.' It has a lot of meaning to them. 'Cunt' reflects an attitude toward the object. So what I wanted to do was investigate that relationship between violent-sexual and violent-nonsexual, sexual and nonsexual words."

"You could do it in several languages."

"Well, there *is* an advantage to doing it in at least two languages. Of course, the control is the critical thing. To have an adequate control."

"Control of what?"

"Experimental control, of whatever you're investigating. And one way of controlling that is to hold the length or duration of the words, and the intensity of the speech, about the same. The content that the word is carrying will be the independent variable that you're changing. But even more interesting would be to substantiate the same results in the second language, where the properties of the word are completely different. That would eliminate whatever possible effects the physical characteristics of the phrases would have."

"That's a linguist's dream."

"Right. It washes them out. The major thing is to see if there's some relationship between these words and pupillary response."

"You imply that these words would activate their fantasy, which is a visual construct, and then alter the pupil's size?"

"Well, I don't know the mechanism—and I don't care. I don't need to know the relationship. What I'm looking for is: Is there a relationship? We can always tease out what it might be later on. But the implication is indeed that those things that are arousing do cause dilatation."

"Do they?"

"If I knew the answer, I wouldn't do the study. I'm interested, first of all, in demonstrating this with normals, and then extending it to deviates. As long as the words mean those things to the individuals, I believe that it's a better measure of their attitude. You can always lie about how you feel, but if the words still maintain their power, or if they can be altered by treatment, that's fascinating. I'm always looking for an objective measure of internal processes. What is *really* happening inside? I don't know. But I can hear the words."

The lab technician, Ted Taylor, has been working while Dr. Sachs and I speak. He addresses Dr. Sachs:

"A friend of mine has been using a pupillometer for a

long time. It gave me a great idea. We should pick out these phrases that we have on the cards. Short, very sharp sentences."

"We already did that, Ted."

"We didn't do it with the pupillometer. We only did it with erection."

"We didn't do it with the pupillometer? But we have it on tape, don't we?"

"Uh huh."

"I put them on tape myself."

"Those are probably too long. You used the whole sentence. We should keep it to a couple of seconds to have an impact."

"The truth is, they're still too complicated to measure pupil size. You need very discrete words. The more words you use, the more variables you're dealing with . . . I suspect that certain words have power in them. Words with sexual connotations. If you present individuals with various scenes describing their deviant behavior, you'll find that there are points at which they become aroused. The word might be a small phrase, like 'beating up a real cunt.' That helps describe the action. 'Feeling her soft breasts . . .' As you're describing certain words, they get erections. We know that anything associated with accelerating erections is highly charged. These words are highly charged. They are powerful at generating erection responses. A word like 'breast' might cause that initial sort of response, because there is a reflex of the pupil to the auditory stimulus."

"As a linguist, you know, I wonder if a word like 'breast' is erotic in itself. When you leaf through a dictionary, you don't get an erection . . ."

"Well, it's not a question we have to philosophize about. We put it on the tape and we record."

"Yet if the word 'breast' were qualified—as 'bare breast'

—or activated in a structure—as 'I'm squeezing her breast'—it might have more of a chance of generating arousal. Figuratively, 'breast' is a source of nourishment, or the seat of the affections; synecdochically, it designates the part of the body between the shoulders, neck, and abdomen; metonymically, the part of a garment that covers the breast; metaphorically, anything resembling the breast in position or form, such as the front of a moldboard, or the face of a tunnel; idiomatically, it connotes the disclosure of a secret, as in 'making a clean breast of' . . ."

"Listen. It would be very easy to see whether or not single words have power in them by taking a look at some neutral words—some sexual words and some words that have a meaning, but not a sexual meaning. All we have to do is to throw in the blank screen. We put the words through the audio and record the pupil size. We could set it at one second, if we could get it to trip as soon as the word appears. What we really need, Ted, is for Bill Bell to tell us how to convert onto the polygraph the sound of the words, so that we can demarcate the beginning and end of the word. We'd plot that on one channel, while we'd put on another channel the pupillometer's response and correlate the two. That's what we really need. Don't you think, Ted?"

"Uh huh."

"If we had a set of words on tape that came on for ten seconds, just repetitions of the word—'breast, breast, breast' . . ."

"And then we stop and record from that?"

"No. You record *while* the word is coming through."

"Okay, sure. You're bound to get some sort of stimulus response—either a loading or unloading of understanding the word in the head; and that'll be reflected in the pupil. The eye would constrict and then dilate, then stabilize every time you would say 'breast' . . . So we'd be getting essentially the same thing we're getting now when we show them a slide and have a reflex period of about three seconds. I think if we were to note any changes, we would see them in that stabilization period."

"But that's within the ten-second period."

"No. I'm saying, just give the stimulus once and then . . ."

"And then record the ten seconds. Of course. I see how it can be done. We must have a bunch of words lined up right on top of each other with a second between them. You hold the pause button on the audio. Then you set up the pupillometer. Put the cumulative integrator at seven-second cycling. You record for seven seconds. Then you release the pause button. The word comes out, and you release the cumulative integrator for another ten seconds. As soon as the word is stopped, you stop the cumulative. Then you hold the cumulative down and present the word again. We could actually do a pretty nice experiment."

"What if you put the key word in neutral and randomize the presentation?"

"Ted, that's the whole *idea*. Have a series of words that are powerful and not powerful, sexual or not sexual . . ."

"Okay, I see your point. But how did this idea about words come about?"

"The professor here is a semanticist, a specialist in words. He's working with a group of analysts and he may help us figure out how to set up our language experiment."

"Yes. I'm quite fascinated by the relation between language and sexuality. Language intensifies sexuality; it may also kill it."

"That's a very good distinction. From my own experience I know that the word destroys the intensity. At times it also helps intensify it, or redirect it."

"I assume that you want to intensify the word in order to 'destroy' the sexual experience that goes with it. It's an exciting idea, quite arousing—I mean, intellectually."

"Let me turn the tables on you now, Professor. What have you learned here that would be of help to me? That's an open-ended question."

"I have to admit that I have some qualms as to the advisability of transforming people's behavior in general, unless, of course, there is a drastic need for it, which is apparently the case here at the clinic—although what people are willing to do, or taught to do, or forced to do, or reluctant to do, is not always a proof that they should actually do it, or that one should actually help them in doing it, even if society expects people to behave in a certain way."

"I'm not sure I'm following you. What advice would you have to offer from your vantage point regarding the patients' arousal to erotic words?"

"Some linguists are investigating the psychological basis of phonation in order to prove that there is a natural relationship between the sounds in language and mental contents. Tenderness expresses itself mostly through consonants like *l* or *m*, which correspond to the sucking movement of the lips, whereas a more aggressive attitude multiplies the occlusives *k*, *t*, and *r*, which denote anger, spite, or repugnance through a spasmodic contraction and a hardening of the laryngeal muscles. Actually, *r*, which is produced *erecta ad palatum lingua*, is always associated with phallic violence. The same phenomena are said to exist in the language of chimpanzees, and, significantly, of Tibetans. It would be easy to check this polarization in more than one language by using, as you suggested, words that are sexual and nonsexual, meaningful and not meaningful . . . Mr. Taylor, Dr. Sachs has implied that we could try that right away."

"Well, sure, we could test that immediately."

"Would you test it on yourself?"

"On myself? Never. Are you crazy?"

"How about testing it on me?"

3

Behave

"**D**o you have any idea what this treatment does to your patients' heads? If you manage to eradicate what turned them on before, do you know at what cost? And are you sure that the pressure you put on one area isn't going to affect them somewhere else? After all, you may very well cure someone of a sadistic arousal, but then something else might pop up instead. He may become a voyeur, a rapist, or a psychiatrist."

"You're talking about symptom substitution. That's an old concept, an old fear that dealing with the symptoms specifically would generate all sorts of weird things. But that has never been supported. I can see that particularly well in these individuals, because that's exactly what I do. I eliminate one arousal pattern. Now, I do notice that when they have multiple arousal patterns of deviant nature—not just one, but multiple, which is the case of about 50 percent of the cases we see—if we destroy the thing that's bothering them the most, they will shift to attending something that's less severe. But that's no big surprise: that's exactly what we hoped they would do."

"What turns each individual on is very singular. It's the way they desire that makes them what they are."

"The patient that I saw last night is attracted to women —their appearance, their hair, their buttocks, their breasts. He enjoys their freshness, but he is very, very interested in their buttocks, in their . . ."

"Ass."

"Their ass, yes. To the extent that when he masturbates in public, he focuses almost exclusively on the woman's ass."

"You mean, when he actually sees one? It's not a fantasy?"

"No. He goes into public places, gets on buses, covers his penis with his coat, and masturbates while looking at women's asses. Now, what's erotic to him is very much what's erotic to you or others. He hasn't cornered the market on what he finds erotic. And yet there's an arousal pattern that is very specific in terms of its magnitude. His nondeviant fantasy involves an excessive amount of touching the woman's ass, feeling the curvature of her ass —and that's perfectly all right. I encourage him to do that. I don't want to destroy his arousal to women's asses. I wouldn't want to do that. What I want to do is change his arousal to women's asses to such an extent that he's not masturbating on the bus with his hands on his penis underneath his coat, which can get him arrested."

"If he were masturbating at home . . ."

"That's okay. You're not going to get arrested for that. I'm all for him dating women with nice asses. I know that's something he's always been aroused to. I know it would be very tough to eliminate. I simply would like him to focus on the woman's ass that he's feeling in bed."

"So 'deviance' is just a bit more deviant than normal."

"A *lot* more deviant. If you measure the arousal pattern of males to young children, you'll find that almost all males have some degree of arousal to them. The difference is quantitative, not qualitative."

"Perversions have no grammar of their own then? Nothing specific?"

"Nothing specific."

"You don't seem to be dealing with the unconscious very much. You target behavior directly—where the law lets off, so to speak. That's quite a shortcut."

"I would hope it's a shortcut. It better be, because what we need is intensive treatment. I'm very cost-conscious as a therapist."

"Because your research is funded?"

"No, because people can't afford therapy, except in New York, Chicago, Los Angeles. In the real world, most patients need something that's cost-efficient. The therapist has to accommodate his therapy to the patient, not the other way around. I'm treating a fellow right now, a private patient, who's had six years of orthodox psychoanalysis. Six years!"

"Did it help?"

"Ha! Why do you think he's seeing me? No, it didn't help him, and he's pretty perturbed about it. His family has laid out a tremendous amount of money. He began analysis at the age of eight in New York. It's only in New York that you can begin analysis at age eight! He was in analysis for three years, stopped and restarted at age sixteen. Four days a week, for three more years, before stopping. He happens to be an exhibitionist, a public masturbator, and he's very young. He's about twenty-two now. You can imagine how much money his family spent. If he was going to change his appointment, he had to give six months' advance notice. Six months' notice!" Dr. Sachs laughs derisively. "And if his therapist couldn't find a patient to replace him, he had to pay for that appointment anyway."

"Was that part of the therapy?"

"That's what the therapist said. But what do *you* think? I think it's bullshit! . . . I'm sure the therapist truly believed it was part of the therapy, however."

"Sure. He's a colleague . . . Were you ever interested in that kind of therapy yourself?"

"Yes, it was the major kind of therapy in my residence. Short psychotherapy though, dynamically oriented, not psychoanalysis per se. Using psychoanalytically based principles. There was nothing else."

"How did you happen to modify your goals so drastically?"

"The change *was* drastic. I realized that without evidence to measure response to treatment, psychiatry becomes an issue of faith. And who knows then? So I started studying the areas in which measurement was possible. That's how I got into behavioral. That's what behavioral means, that you can measure objectively what you do. I became a behaviorist in order to stay in psychiatry."

"I thought behavioral meant primarily modifying behavior."

"The behaviorists have been, I think, misunderstood. Most people believe that behaviorists deal exclusively with behavior. That is not the case. Actually, with this treatment, I'm not dealing with behavior at all. The behaviorism that I am most comfortable with is called 'the experimental analysis of behavior.' It has nothing to do with behavior therapy, it has to do with evaluation. It has to do with how you assess response to treatment, or need for treatment.

"The way behaviorism deals with reports of thoughts is what they call 'self-statements,' which we also use. And indeed, there are a number of off-shoots of behaviorism, called 'cognitive behavior therapy,' which deal primarily with subjective statements . . .

"I really don't care about the theoretical position that people would like to identify me with. I think it's irrelevant. The critical thing is that you are able to delineate what therapy involves to the extent that you can tell another person how to do the therapy, and that they can carry it out without any special knowledge."

"Very pragmatic."

"Pragmatic, yeah."

"Your treatment may not be called 'behavior therapy,' but it still is a form of behavior modification."

"Well, a lot of things are called 'behavior modification.' "

"Don't you modify behavior?"

"I should hope so. No therapist is interested in simply changing internal thought. He wants to alter the expression of that thought. It's the outward behavior that gets these people into trouble. That's what they need to change, ultimately, and that's true of whatever kind of therapy you're talking about."

"Could you get the same kind of evaluation through some form of ongoing psychoanalysis?"

"You may be able to identify what is erotic to an individual through analysis. My way is just to measure the sexual arousal, directly."

"You would still agree with Freud, I suppose, that sexuality is at the root of most psychic disorders."

"Oh, I don't know about that. I'm a sex researcher, so I evaluate sexual issues. But my belief is that, although many patients may have a dynamic ideology, after they have been going with their deviant arousal for five years, the ideology becomes irrelevant. The behavior itself is highly reinforcing."

"You're reinforcing it in a different way."

"I'm just dealing with symptoms, because that's what they got arrested for. You see, too much time has been spent in the psychological area, trying to delineate—tease apart—various subelements of treatment. Less time has been spent in determining effective therapies. Much of the current research deals with 'Why does it work?' as opposed to 'Does it work?' I think we have to spend some more time determining that it does work before we try and tease out why it works. I am a person who is primarily interested in documenting the effectiveness of treatment with some objective measure. That may be an error on my part, but, then, that's a limitation that I have."

"Is pleasure actually transferred from the deviant model to a more 'positive' arousal?"

"Well, initially it isn't. If a person has been interested in four-year-old girls all his life and you teach him a technology of arousal to adult women, at first it isn't as exciting. What you do as a therapist is encourage him to hold on and wait, to allow the arousal to nondeviant objects to become stronger. That's what therapy is all about—dealing with the resistances to change. The treatment itself is rather simple, but getting the patient to do it, and to do it right, is more complicated. Most of the therapy involves pointing out to the patients why it is in their best interest to stop this arousal pattern, to eliminate it."

"You persuade them to tolerate some kind of self-mutilation."

"Well, this is what happens when you devise a successful method. First people say, 'Why don't you give them an effective treatment? Find something that really works!'

Then you give them something that's really effective, and people say, 'Oh, my goodness, this is really terrible!' "

"What's upsetting is the idea that one can persuade people that it is in their best interest to be modified."

"Some people drop out of therapy. The patient says, 'I'm aroused to kids, I like being aroused to kids, and I don't want to do anything about it. See you!' That happens, sometimes. Actually, I'm trying to design the therapy so that it happens less frequently."

"What's the proportion of dropouts?"

"Well, of 324 referred patients, 199 actually entered treatment. Of the 199 we've treated, 65 percent finished the program; and of those 199 patients, 194 have been child molesters."

"Why so many child molesters?"

"We've got a grant to treat them. This is one of the few free clinics that treat child molesters. The private clinics cost, and of those, I would estimate that less than ten, maybe five, are doing the kind of treatment we are. It started only six years ago. Even though they might not use this kind of technology, more and more therapists are aware of the techniques we use, or should be. We came here, to Chicago, on a three-year grant to treat a large group of child molesters. We have people from across the country come in, from as far away as Texas. But of course most of our patients are from the Chicago area. And some from New York. We do a follow-up at six and twelve months."

"How many patients are willing to be followed up after the cure?"

"The big fall-off is early in treatment. Once they get post-treatment, they stay with us, especially if they get to six months. Of course, we don't have a follow-up on 100 percent of the people, because it's a voluntary program. Of those that we were able to follow up, we have 82 percent stop their deviant behavior. At twelve months, it was 69 percent. So there's roughly 70 percent stopped deviance. That's pretty high."

"Let's see . . . But out of the 199 who began the program, that's really only about 45 percent after twelve months."

"Well, yes . . . The total treatment lasts thirty weeks. They go into group treatment once a week for an hour and a half. I run them in the lab again after ten weeks, twenty weeks, and at the end. So, all in all, they get their lab run three times."

"There's no more treatment during the follow-up?"

"No. If you're doing research and you set a design, you have to stop the treatment in order to find out how effective it is. Then you look to whether or not they recommit crimes. We've treated nineteen different groups. All the data is not yet in. Now we're investigating whether we can predict recidivism or recommission of crime on the basis of the erection measure."

"And if they recommit crimes, what do you do?"

"They enter what is known as the 'mini-group.' That's all our failures." Dr. Sachs laughs. "Actually, we haven't had *enough* recommissions of crimes . . . It's a funny statement, but in order to evaluate the effectiveness of treatment, we need to look at those who do, and those who don't, and we didn't get that."

"I'm still curious as to the long-term effect of this treatment."

"It might be unrealistic to think that we can take somebody into the lab and change behavioral patterns that have existed for ten years with a ten-week conditioning program. Some studies have shown, however, that with the proper follow-up and booster sessions, it is possible for people to maintain these changes. If you follow these people up and continually measure their sexual arousal, when the problem starts to reappear, you give another, shorter

series of deconditioning sessions. People need to be reinforced. You have a new person that goes out. And this new
person needs to see that the stuff he's learned really works.
Sexual contacts with adult females is something they
never had before, just interaction with children. So they
need some successes there. And as you know, when we
approach a woman, we're not always reinforced for it.
We're sometimes rejected quite violently and we feel bad
about the whole thing. We don't know if we're socially
desirable anymore. That applies to everything. You won't
get what you've been trained to expect. Sometimes it
works, sometimes it doesn't."

"That means a lifelong follow-up."

"It might mean a lifelong follow-up. The analogy is with
alcoholics who need to be constantly reminded that they
can't control their drinking. You prevent relapse through
a therapeutic support system."

"What conclusions can you draw from your results so
far?"

"Well, for whatever reason, incest cases are the easiest
to treat. Our highest success rate was with them. They
rarely reoffend. Next easiest to treat were those who tar-
geted young girls. Next, boys. But if it's crimes against boys
—not very young ones, but the adolescent boys—then
they have a very high likelihood of recommitting crimes.
We found that the individuals who continued the behavior
were mostly homosexual child molesters. As it happens,
the people who committed the most crimes before treatment committed the most crimes afterwards. Big surprise,
ha!"

"How do you explain their resistance to treatment?"

"This is the hardest group to work with because they're
obsessively involved, exclusively involved with children.
Pedophiles who are aroused by adults as well have other
references. They're not losing *everything*. Once the person

gets beyond the morality involved, the real issue for the individual is: Well, if I lose my arousal, I lose my entire sexual identity. That's why he resists much more. Most of the time they don't even come for treatment. And the question is: Can you treat them? Because if they don't believe that there is a problem, then I don't see how you can treat them. Child molesters have a compulsive behavior. More so than rapists, who are differently motivated. Some rape for sexual reasons, some for power reasons, and some for anger reasons. In child molesters, the sexual component is more important, more specific."

"What's the proportion of homosexual child molesters in your program?"

"Less than half our patients have crimes against boys."

"How do you explain that homosexual offenders are more likely to persist?"

"They're not homosexual offenders. They're males who target young boys. There isn't a specific treatment for that particular arousal pattern. It's probably because they start their behavior at an earlier age, or that they have more behavior with boys than those who target young girls. And then they pay for sex. They believe that the boys are willing, that they are paying for a service and therefore are not doing anything wrong. The guy I saw the other day is a good example. He's a homosexual pedophile. He's been involved with children all his life. He happens to be turned on to spanking kids ten to thirteen, and sometimes adolescents—not violently, he says, but some of the kids have objected. He pays them money and he prorates it by the degree of force that he uses: two dollars for spanking with clothes on; three dollars with clothes off, light spanking; five dollars for pants down, light spanking; ten dollars for heavy, hard spanking, clothes off."

"That's pretty elaborate."

"Yes. He spent two years in a psychiatric hospsital, supposedly for treatment. While he was there he involved himself fifty or sixty times with ten or twelve boys—while he was in the hospital for treatment! See, the system doesn't work. And why do rapists go free? First of all, less than one-half of rapes are reported. There's a very low incidence of false reporting, so most of these are real. But when the police go out and arrest somebody, the likelihood of that person being found guilty is only 13 percent nationally. The woman, unfortunately, becomes the defendant. The rapist's attorneys attempt to discredit her in the course of the trial. It's a humiliating procedure to go through, so she doesn't press, or she'll drop the charges. It's pretty unusual that someone observed the assault, so evidence becomes an issue. It's just doggone hard to prove. And then there's plea bargaining: in order to avoid lengthy trials, they plea-bargain down to a lesser crime. I tell you, the system just doesn't work. The treatment of sex crimes could be reduced by a program to treat adolescent offenders. Studies indicate that early intervention can successfully steer young people away from deviant behavior. There's only one treatment program for adolescent offenders in the state or the city, and I think it's essential that we have more."

"How do you devise an effective treatment?"

"When I started this treatment, I was using a variety of techniques that we thought were good. But on the basis of the data collected, we realized that they weren't. So we threw them out. We are constantly filtering through the techniques, and keeping the treatments that seem the most effective. When we have one that we really think is good, we apply an appropriate design to quantify just how good it is. And if that holds up, we use it. That's how you design programs."

"How did you happen to switch from aversive techniques to the kind of treatment you're using now?"

"A number of factors led me to this methodology. After doing research in this area for ten years, I had already done almost every form of therapy used to decrease deviant arousal. I had done them all, throwing out practically everything. Covert sensitization was the most effective one left, and it really was very good."

"What's covert sensitization?"

"It means pairing and associating aversive scenes with the deviant scenes, so that they take on a negative tone. I have done a research project using covert sensitization, so I'm no amateur at it. I do good covert. I also did an investigation on how to alter masturbation fantasy, and therefore alter arousal patterns, using a switching process, going from deviant to nondeviant to deviant to nondeviant.

"Then I met with Dr. William Marshall, from Kingston, Ontario, who had devised this new technique. I used it on some of the people who had already finished the best forms of therapy that *I* had. And yet his treatment could take the people that the covert didn't touch and really help them. That's why I moved to using Dr. Marshall's technique. I don't do much covert sensitization anymore, simply because it's very expensive.

"Actually, I did one recently on a very dangerous fellow who was heavy into sadomasochistic fantasies. I mean bad ones. Hitting the woman over the head with a baseball bat, cutting up her face to disfigure it . . ."

"Did he actually *do* that?"

"No, these are fantasies, but he was losing control, and that's why he came to the clinic. He had gone to rape a woman and couldn't get into her building. He felt he was going overboard. He was afraid he was going to harm his family. He had hit his brother across the face with a baseball bat and knocked his teeth out. His family feared for their safety. A very dangerous fellow. He used to shoot at cats in his yard with a shotgun. I felt pretty uncomfortable treating him.

"I associated his sadomasochistic scenes with fantasy images of an aversive nature, such as, 'And you're strangling the woman. You see yourself right there. You feel your hands around her neck, you're strangling her and choking her, you're going to kill her . . .' Then cut to: 'You see your mother. She's being raped. She's being raped by a relative of the woman that you raped and tried to murder. They're getting revenge. You see your mother, they're holding her down and she's screaming, "It isn't me who did it, it was Billy, my son!" And they don't care. They're going to rape her in retaliation. And you see her face, she's screaming, "It wasn't me, it was my son!" And they say, "We know, lady" . . .'

"You see, when you move back and forth from the deviant to that covert scene to the deviant—covert, deviant, covert—it teaches the individual how to pull that scene into his mind when he has urges to rape. I gave him eighteen hours of covert sensitization, and it reduced his arousal somewhat. But—gee whiz!—it didn't touch him too much. So I used the present technique with him for about thirty-six hours, and just destroyed his arousal.

"I did a one-hour telephone follow-up on him this morning—he lives halfway across the United States—and in the midst of the interview I spilled coffee all over my desk. I had to clean up the mess while talking to him."

"Did the therapy work on him?"

"His family reported that he's no longer violent. It stopped, all of it. They're really impressed by that. However, I don't find covert sensitization cost-efficient. The guy I saw last night, who was turned on to women's asses, had four hours of therapy at home for every hour of my contact with him."

"The patient takes over the therapy. . . "

"*That's* cost-efficient. And it's helpful for the patient to see that he can indeed take charge of his life, because that's how he feels."

"Ideally, then, there would be no therapist in this treatment. Everybody would be curing themselves at home."

"Well, it doesn't work that way."

"That would be the most cost-efficient. You could process people through a lab once a year, once in a lifetime, or at birth."

"I would agree with you, yes, that would be the best thing. All therapists know, however, that people can't change themselves, especially those who are so entranced by their own fantasies. Nor can they assess their response to treatment. Many of them lie."

"*That's* taking charge of their lives, isn't it?"

"Well, no. What led me to this methodology, however, essentially had to do with the ethical issues. For instance, if you use apomorphine to averse people, it gives them nausea, it causes them to vomit. They can get really sick if they take too much of it. And if you do that, you're open to charges of ethical abuse, just like with electrical aversion providing pain associated with children."

"I thought electrical aversion was still currently being used as a therapy."

"In some places it is, and this is an ethical issue. More importantly, it's a political issue. As a matter of fact, you can design electrical aversion treatments that are not coercive at all. We used to administer them years ago, where the patient determined whether they gave themselves shocks or not, and at what level. We showed them how to use the technology, but it was up to them to do the treatment. You *can* design treatments that are free of ethical abuse, but if the society still believes that there is no way to do this, then you have to bend to the nonreality of the majority of people."

"The 'nonreality of the majority'? That's an interesting concept."

"I mean, that if these people did the treatment and saw

that it wasn't any big deal, then they would change their perceptions. But right now, they envision *A Clockwork Orange*, do they not? It's a very colorful, beautifully directed movie, which the public associates with aversive therapy, but . . ."

"You don't recognize yourself there?"

"No, because that treatment was done without consent."

"Is that the main difference?"

"Well, consent is definitely the critical issue."

"Not the technology that's being used?"

"No, it's the consent."

"The same technique without consent would, I believe, be called torture. Electricity, after all, is widely used to extract information . . ."

"Wait a minute! Wait a minute! If you know the advantages and disadvantages of this 'torture,' if you're not under coercion to participate, and if there's some person who oversees whether this is ethically acceptable, then I don't see anything wrong with it. People agree to undergo pain. We call it surgery."

"Some people get pleasure from pain. We call them masochists."

"We can treat masochists with electrical aversion."

"Really? In spite of the fact that they enjoy pain?"

"Yes, yes."

"Isn't that somewhat contradictory?"

"That's only contradictory in your mind. I don't get entangled in a philosophical viewpoint. You try to explain it from your conception, I look at it empirically. I say, let's carry out an experiment with a masochist using a pain-initiated treatment and see the outcome. And what I find is that it doesn't preclude successful therapy. But we have other ways of treating sexual deviates now, and they are much more effective."

4
Enjoy

t's February 3, and it's six o'clock. I'm in bed with Margaret. We've just been out for the evening. We really enjoy being with each other. Now we're lying together in bed experiencing the warmth of each other's bodies. I'm running my hands over her body, over her breasts, over her soft full breasts, over her nipples, feeling the warmth of her vagina. She is gently stroking my chest with one hand, rubbing my penis lightly with her other hand. I feel the warmth of her hands on my body. Very enjoyable. Very exciting. And both my hands over her breasts, over her vagina.

The warmth of her body really turns me on. I'm really

*getting excited, really turned on. Now I'm going to lick
her vagina. She's spreading her legs and I'm licking her
vagina, and around her clitoris. I'm really getting
turned on licking her vagina, and she enjoys it, it turns
her on. I feel her working her way across the bed. Her
legs tightly around my head, she has her hand on my
head. She puts her hands on my head to guide me, to
guide my tongue to where she wants it.*

"Is that the new treatment?"

"Yes. It has to do with the structure and fabrication of
fantasies. In a nutshell, it goes like this: when you are
small and you are aroused and feeling pleasure, you think
of various experiences, random thoughts about what
you've been doing that day. Those thoughts are brought to
mind during masturbation and orgasm, pleasurable experiences. But, of course, your perceptual apparatus is highly
idiosyncratic, highly individualized. As time goes by, you
recall some of those early sexual experiences better than
others because they are so vivid to you.

"Now let's say that item number 2 on this graph was the
sexual experience that was remembered with greater ease
and recalled with greater frequency once associated and
paired with sexual arousal, masturbation, and orgasm, so
that it becomes more powerful. Let's say that item number
1 wasn't really exciting, or wasn't a true early experience;
it is recalled less and less with orgasm, and so it loses its
punch. And let's say that item number 3 is recalled about
the same. Because number 2 has been recalled more times,
it is linked in hundreds of ways with pleasurable experiences."

"It is reinforced."

"Yes."

*She's really excited, moving around on the bed. I feel
my tongue licking her vagina and thighs, over her cli-*

toris. She really enjoys it. I am licking her vagina and I'm rubbing my hands up over her breasts, over her breasts and stomach. I can feel her legs tighten around my head. She's really getting excited. She's really moving around, it feels very good to her and really excites me.

Now she's going to suck my penis. Really warm now, around my penis. It feels so exciting to me, really good, I'm really excited now, really excited. She licks my penis. She's sucking my penis and it feels good to me. I rub my hands over her back and over her ass. She's lying down and I'm rubbing my hands over her back. She really enjoys that, it relaxes her. She likes to feel my warm hands on her back. I'm liking the warmth of her body. I rub my hands over her back, over her ass, really getting turned on.

"Item number 2 becomes exceedingly powerful, while number 3 remains its same old self in terms of its strength, and number 1, because it's never recalled, trails off and disappears. I believe that's the way sexual arousal develops—and that's the key to altering it."

"Is there a capacity for sexual innovation?"

"Oh, absolutely. There may be elements of number 2 which have a particular interest to you. So it may develop an additional variety, and this might be number 4, which cleaves off from number 2. It's a new twist on something that's remembered better. So, innovation? Absolutely.

"Here's the way you usually fantasize: you think of something that's highly erotic and you dwell on it for a while. Then you'll go to something else that will also be highly erotic, so you'll dwell a little bit on that. That's what normally happens: you never focus on the fantasy too long, you move off from it, you skip real fast to another fantasy to maintain your arousal."

I'm licking around her ass and legs, feeling the warmth of her body. I lick around her anus, and it turns her on, gets her excited. I rub my hands over her back, over her ass. I'm really excited, turned on. Licking all around her ass. Now she's going to turn over and she's going to guide my penis into her vagina. She has her hands on my penis. She's guiding my penis into her vagina now.

Her vagina is wet. I slide it in and out, in and out of her vagina and it really feels very, very exciting to me. I feel her warm body under me. I feel her arms tight around me and her hands on my back. I feel her hands on my back, running down over my back, down, over my ass. I feel my penis moving in and out of her vagina and it really feels very, very good and I hear her saying how good it feels.

"Now, what if you want to destroy number 2? How do you do it? There are all sorts of ways; but the system that we have found to be the most effective works in this way. We want you to begin fantasizing what we call a nondeviant sexual experience with an adult—consenting sex. An experience that involves mutual participation."

She's spreading her legs and pulling her legs back, way back, and wrapping her legs around me. I feel my penis penetrating deep, deep inside her vagina. Now I hear her asking me to pump harder, pump harder, because she really, really enjoys it. And I feel her hands running down my back and over my ass, and that feels very, very good, very exciting to me. I feel my penis deep, deep inside her vagina, and it feels really very good, very exciting to me. Feel her hands on me. I'm sliding my penis in and out, in and out of Margaret's vagina. She's holding her arms tight around me, it feels very warm, very exciting to me, it feels very, very good, very exciting to me, to have my penis in Margaret's vagina. As I move up and down upon her I feel her warm hands on my back, rubbing my back, and I feel her legs wrapped around my legs.

"If you have difficulty fantasizing, then you might think of adults that you have seen recently that you would like to have a sexual experience with, or experiences that you've actually had. You will masturbate on the parts that are the most exciting for you, to get as aroused as possible."

I feel my penis inside her vagina, penetrating deep inside. I'm really turned on, I'm excited. With my penis deep inside her warm vagina, I feel her warm breasts on my chest. I'm really turned on and excited. She's enjoying it too and she's moving her hands over my back. I hear her say how good it feels. I'm moving my penis in and out of her vagina, feeling her breasts, feeling my penis inside her vagina, and I'm going to ejaculate . . .

"And you ejaculate as rapidly as possible. How long does it take you to masturbate to ejaculation? Let's say it's five minutes. Then we add two minutes to that: it makes a total of seven. This is the switch-point that we don't want you to go beyond using this nondeviant fantasy. After you ejaculate, or after seven minutes have passed, whichever comes first, you immediately start using your child-molestation fantasy for the rest of the hour. Postorgasm."

It's in the future now. I have already found control over my fantasies. I don't have deviant thoughts anymore. They're all normal, healthy fantasies. But just once I think it'd be nice to have one about rape. One couldn't hurt.

" 'One couldn't hurt . . .' This is what you tell yourself before getting into the actual behavior. We'll use that as a 'trap.' Obviously we don't want you to use the deviant fantasy the way you used it in the past. In the past, you were not running your life. These fantasies were running your life. Whenever you used them, it got you into trouble. Now you are going to use these fantasies to gain control over your behavior so that you won't get arrested. The way to do that, the most fascinating way known at this time, is this particular technique. But you have to do it correctly. You have to do it properly."

I'm following this woman. It's night and I see that she has gone into a house. I wait till she opens the door and then I rush up. I force my way in behind her. Then I grab her and throw her down. I point a knife at her and tell her that I won't hurt her if she does what I say, but she better do what I say and not make any noise.

"What is different from the way the patient has used these deviant fantasies in the past? Here is what's different: In the past you flipped from one element to another during masturbation, you allowed the fantasy to move forward rapidly, dwelling just a short time on the very erotic parts. You ejaculated, and that was that. You used this fantasy for five minutes, and then you refiled it. When you bring the fantasy back again, you're likely to bring another fantasy along with it, and you'll run that one through too. So there's never any real opportunity for satiation. You won't extinguish that arousal pattern because it's never presented long enough.

"We don't want you to do it that way anymore. Instead, we want you to destroy your interest in whatever is the most exciting part of the fantasy by going over that part during the period of masturbation. Let's say you are out on a beach. There's a young boy with you, an eight-year-old. You are putting your hands down his swimming trunks, feeling his penis. Let's say that out of all that, the part that is the most erotic is moving your hands into his swimsuit. That's the element that really turns you on. Instead of describing an elaborate fantasy like you might have used in the past, we want you, once you've ejaculated, to dwell on just the element that is the most erotic. So you would say: 'I'm with this eight-year-old boy at the beach; I'm putting my hands down his swimming suit to feel his penis. He really wants me to. I see him there and I'm feeling his penis because he wants me to.' While you continue to masturbate, you will repeat that part, incessantly.

"Why? Why do you need to do that? Because it is these kinds of elements that lead you to involving yourself with children. If you can eliminate this factor in your head, you will gain control over your behavior."

I tell her to take her clothes off. She is naked now, lying on the floor naked. It really turns me on. I want to rape her. I really want to have her body. I'm thinking that I'm not doing anything wrong, that I'm not really hurting her, that she could enjoy it if she wanted to. And nothing's going to happen. I won't be caught, I'm too smart for that. But those are all lies. I am raping this woman. I pushed her down and made her take her clothes off. I am making her spread her legs wide apart. I want to embarrass her, humiliate her, really hurt her. I want to satisfy myself sexually. I don't care what she thinks about making love to me. I just want to have her body.

"I want you to throw out, not incorporate, things that you're thinking about, like, 'Gee, I better not do this because I'm going to be arrested.' I don't want you to have those kinds of fantasies during the deviant section, because I only want to include there those parts that we wish to eliminate your arousal to."

I'm going to rape this woman, but I don't know why. I just want to rape her, and hurt her, make her feel bad. And I am making her take her clothes off, forcing this woman to take her clothes off. She is begging me not to, not to rape her. I can hear her saying, "Please," she doesn't want me to do it. But I'm forcing her to take her clothes off. And now she's naked before me, this woman that I am raping, is naked in front of me, and I am forcing her to, forcing this woman to spread her legs apart.

"You know, if you do something that you enjoy doing, and if you do that to excess, it destroys your interest in the thing. This treatment, this training, this method you're learning here can provide you control over your deviant fantasies. It goes like this: you take the part that is deviant and highly erotic and you go over it again and again and again and again and again and again and again and again and again and again and again and again, until it is really *boring*."

I'm violent, really violent. I am licking her vagina. I am licking her vagina and it really turns me on, turns me on to be licking her vagina, forcing her to do those things, raping her. I really enjoy raping this woman. It really turns me on even though I am hurting her, because there's nothing she can do about it. She can't fight me; I'm too powerful for her. I am raping her and I don't care if she likes it or not. I'm going to fool my mind, I'm going to fool my mind and think that I don't care. I'm going to fool my mind and think that I'm not really doing anything wrong, that I'm not really hurting her. I'm going to make myself think that it is not really me that is raping her. It is not really me but another part of me that I don't know, that I don't recognize. I'm going to make myself believe that I would not rape anybody. And I am licking the vagina of this woman that I am raping. There's nothing she can do about it. I am in control. I am in control of the situation. Nothing's going to happen. I'm going to rape her. I'm not thinking about the consequences, of what may happen, of how this will affect her, and how it will affect me. I won't get caught. I'm not hurting her, nothing bad will happen to her. It's what I'm making myself believe. I don't care about the future. It doesn't matter because I'm not going to get caught.

"You might say, 'I can't do it, because if I ejaculated at the switch-point, after seven minutes, I can't ejaculate again. I can't even masturbate, because I don't have an erection.' But you need to go ahead and attempt to masturbate using the deviant fantasies, even if it's difficult for you. Because what will happen? First of all, difficulty will now be associated with your use of these fantasies. Second, they aren't going to be so erotic because you just got through ejaculating. Third, if you have been masturbating, or attempting to masturbate, for ten, twenty, thirty, forty, fifty minutes, it's a very dull experience. And, of course, that's exactly what you want these fantasies to be. Dull and uninteresting."

I like being in control. She can't fight me. I'm too powerful for her. There's nothing she can do. I am raping her and there's nothing that can stop me. I am really enjoying licking her vagina, it's really turning me on. I don't care if she doesn't like it. All that matters is that I enjoy myself, have a good time. After all I'm not hurting her. I'm doing her no wrong.

"Some people, when they first start the treatment, ejaculate. They switch over to the deviant fantasy, and then they ejaculate again. What do you do then? Don't worry about it. Just keep using the deviant fantasy over and over again. No problem. The usual individual, after three or four hours, doesn't have this recurrent ejaculation problem."

I don't care about her. I beat her. I just want to have a good time. I'm licking her vagina over and over again. It's turning me on because I'm really raping her. I'm just thinking about myself and how good it feels. I don't care about her, don't care about her at all. She doesn't matter. So I continue raping her until I'm through. I'm not thinking about her. Just thinking about how good it feels right now. I know I'm not going to get caught. I'm too smart for that. They'll never catch me and I'll rape as many times as I feel like it. They'll never catch me.

5

Date

Dr. Sachs teaches social skills to one of his patients:

"Just let your arms go limp. And you might want to turn that chair so you can put your back up, kind of in the corner. I'm trying to get you as comfortable as possible. Just relax, relax your whole body. Just get it completely relaxed. You can stick out your legs if you'd like. Does that help? And maybe you want to lean your head up against that box or something? How's that?

"Now, is there any kind of scene or situation that's particularly relaxing for you? A beautiful mountain scene? What would the mountain scene look like? Heavily forested? A small, refreshing stream going through it? You'd be by yourself? Out of doors? Up in the mountains?

"You just see this scene, okay? Put yourself in that scene. You're seeing yourself right there, very calm and relaxed. No one around. Very calm and relaxed. Now, I want you to tighten your shoulder muscles. Relax and concentrate on the feelings going through your body. Very calm and relaxed. Tighten up the muscles of your neck. Tighten, tighten. Okay, relax. Concentrate on the sensation of relaxation. Now clench your teeth and close your mouth. Your master muscles on the side of your jaw—clench down, relax. Let that feeling go right on through your body. Calm and relaxed.

"Now, if 10 is as anxious as you can get, and zero is not anxious at all, how anxious are you right now? Just lift your left index finger when I get to the number: 10, 9, 8, 7, 6, 5, 4, 3. Three, okay. Very calm. Calm and relaxed. Just stare up at the mountains. Beautiful scene, mountains in the background, a stream, you can hear the stream. Very calm and relaxed. By yourself. You have time off from work. No rush. Very calm and relaxed. Tighten the muscles around your larynx. Tighten, tighten, now relax, calm. Let that sensation go through the rest of your body. Calm and relaxed . . . 10, 9 . . . 2. Okay, 2.

"You're ready to talk to a woman. You wonder if the muscles are going to tighten up in your neck. You think you may be feeling them tighten up. Very calm and relaxed. How anxious did that scene make you? . . . 10, 9 . . . 4. Okay, 4. Very calm and relaxed. Now, if the scene I present you gives you more than a 3, in terms of your anxiety, immediately get off the scene, and move to the mountains. Just throw up your left index finger and go to the mountains. Otherwise, just imagine the scene as I am describing it.

"Every time you hear a number, relax even more. Three,

very relaxed; 2, very relaxed; 1, very relaxed. Tighten up
the muscles of your larynx. Relax. Relax and let that feeling . . . rest your head back. Calm scene. Calm and relaxed . . .

"You see a woman that you'd like to talk with. You're
walking over to her. As you're walking over to her, you're
wondering if your muscles are going to tighten up in your
neck. You're starting to worry about whether they would
or not. You stay very calm and relaxed. Then you turn to
her, keeping very calm and relaxed . . . And what do you
say to her?"

"Really crowded in here, isn't it?"

"Okay. Calm and relaxed. Up in the mountains, by
yourself, not pressured. Calm and relaxed. You switch
scenes. You see a woman. You'd like to talk to her. You're
walking toward her. You see her right there. Calm and
relaxed. In your mind you're starting to wonder: Are the
muscles in my neck going to tighten up? Stay calm and
relaxed. You turn to her, at a slow rate of speech, low
voice, and you say . . . What would you say?"

"It's really very crowded in here?"

"Uh huh. Very calm and relaxed. Amount of anxiety
you felt? . . . 10, 9 . . . 3. Three, okay. Remember if you go
over 3, go to this calm scene. You're on a mountain, looking across the beautiful stream. It's just perfect for you.
Perfect. You see a woman in a social gathering that you
would like to talk to. You wonder if she's going to reject
you if you stutter. Is she going to want to talk to you? She
thinks maybe you're dumb? Calm scene. Up in the mountain, by yourself, looking across the meadow. Relax the
muscles in your throat. You're reminded of the times that
you've felt rejected because of your stuttering. Is this
woman going to reject you too? Walking over towards
her. Very calm and relaxed. You turn to her and
say . . . What would you say?"

"Really a lively party?"

"Maybe she would reject you. The thought comes in your mind. Calm scene? . . . 10, 9 . . . 4. Okay, 4. Very calm and relaxed. Tighten up the muscles of your larynx. Tighten, tighten, tighten. Now relax and let that feeling go through your body. You're approaching a woman at a party. She's about your age. She's attractive to you. She's about six feet away and you start to think, what if I stutter? Maybe she would reject me because of the stuttering. Relax your laryngeal muscles. Tighten them up. Relax. Tighten. Tighten. Relax. Relax.

"Did you feel your larynx tightening up that last time? If so, lift your left index finger. Uh huh. You did. And I saw it too. Very calm and relaxed. Looking out over the mountains. Switch scenes. You see a woman at a party. She's five feet away. Will she reject you? Stay very calm and relaxed. You turn to her and you say . . . What would you say?"

"Nice party? This is really a fun party?"

"Say it again."

"Really a fun party."

"You can feel relaxed the rest of the day now. Just keeping your larynx completely relaxed. Think of a calm scene. Anxiety now? . . . 10, 9 . . . 2. Okay, 2. Just open your eyes when you feel like it. How'd it go today?

"It's strange that I can see it from right here. I see your larynx, because of your Adam's apple. I saw your larynx move three times today. During that last scene, the one involving rejection. Jim, what you need to learn is how to relax in spite of the thought."

"Uh huh."

"I think that will help because, indeed, in the real world, what you have to learn is how to speak in spite of fear. See? Now what I want you to do is to keep notes on situations that actually occur, because we have to put those, as scenes, right into your therapy. When you feel yourself tightening up, write down what's happening, what's going on in your head."

"Uh huh."

"What's going on in your head."

―――――――

"Let me back up a little bit and talk about behavioral approaches to the deviate's relationship to society.

"You see, behaviorism approaches all problems in terms of excesses or deficits. Everything can be broken down into the absence of a behavior that the individual needs, or the excessive presence of a behavior that the individual does not. Or both, or different combinations, depending on what kind of problem you're talking about."

"Too much arousal and not enough dates."

"Right. Some of the rapists that I see—or some of the child molesters—they don't know how to approach women. They don't know how to initiate or carry out a conversation. They don't know how to keep the flow of communication going. They don't know how to maintain eye contact. They don't know how to select a subject that will be nonthreatening to the woman, so that she'll feel comfortable talking with them without having to reveal a lot about herself. That's a behavioral deficit that they have.

"You might approach it from: How did this person fail to develop this social skill? What was it about their early training that made it difficult for them to do so? And that, in typical therapy, takes a large amount of time. I believe that it should take a very short amount of time. The majority of therapy should not deal with the antecedents of why the patient has this deficit, but should deal directly with teaching him the new skills, and how to apply them in various situations so that what I call 'generalization' occurs. They not only can learn it here, but they can practice it in the real world and become adept at it without being anxious."

"You think that deviations are the result of a social deficit?"

"No, I don't believe that. If you look at any deviant, you'll find that that deviant has excessive deviant arousal. Uh, and that's consistent across all deviations . . . What you would do, in addition to determining the excessive deviant arousal, is look at other possible areas needing treatment. If I'm working with a rapist, and that rapist doesn't have social skills, I believe it behooves me to teach him those skills."

———

"What kinds of situations have come up, Jim, where you might have wanted to initiate a conversation but you didn't, or it was difficult for you, or you may have wondered how to do it?"

"Uh, I . . . I had a chance on the El. It's about the only appropriate chance I ever had. A young woman, about my age, that sat down next to me. She looked, you know, halfway friendly."

"What does that mean, when she's 'halfway friendly'?"

"That she wasn't looking straight ahead with a blank look on her face."

"So what does that say?"

"That she probably wouldn't mind some encounter."

"She *may* not mind. You don't know. It's anyone's guess. But at least she's more likely to be willing to talk with you than if she were looking straight ahead with a blank look and ignoring you completely, right? She's kind of smiling. She's saying, It's all right to initiate a conversation with me. So what did you say?"

"Oh, I didn't . . ."

"Okay, you didn't." He laughs. "That's why you're here, right?" They both laugh. "What were you thinking about?"

The surrogate enters, and the patient turns his chair to face her.

"I had something in mind to talk about. There were some young kids on the El running all around, making lots of noise, disturbing people in the cars. Something ready-made that would have been an easy comment."

"What might you have said?"

Jim remains silent for a moment, then pretends joviality:

"Gee, there are a lot of wild kids running around in the car."

"Let's stop right here. What did you think about that response, Celeste? How did it come across to you?"

She answers in a professional voice: "I thought what you said came across well. It would be better if you get your eye contact first. Wait until something happens and you're both looking at that, then at each other, rather than just saying it."

"How much eye contact did he show you?"

"None, Doctor. So he scared me when he just started talking. No, he didn't scare me, but he jolted me. I wasn't ready for it."

"How much eye contact is appropriate?"

"Well, he could see by how much I'm willing to give him by not looking away."

"How much was she willing to give you just now, Jim?"

"Just now? I would say a fair amount. I know she heard what I said."

"Are you talking about on the El, Jim, or about right here?"

"Right here."

"Did she look at you?"

"Yes."

"Did you look at him, Celeste?"

"Did I look at him, Doctor? On the El?"

"No, right here."

"Oh, right here. No. Just now I wasn't looking at him too much. Maybe he needs to wait until something brings us together."

"Are you talking about before I say . . ."

"No, she doesn't mean . . ."

"What do you mean?"

"I meant before . . ."

"All right, all right. Let's hear five other statements that you could say. Five other comments, or five other ways. Five different times." Dr. Sachs laughs.

"Wild kids!"

"How was that, Celeste?"

"That was . . . all right. It didn't bring me to say anything on it."

"How was the eye contact?"

"Brief. Very brief."

"Brief and acceptable?"

"He looked away too quickly. So he made *me* look away quickly." To Jim: "You know, *I* followed *you*."

"I wonder if that might be all right. Don't you think, Celeste? He's really kind of fishing to see what you're going to say. In Chicago, on the El, that's quite a different story than anywhere else in the world. Here a lot of eye contact might disturb people . . . Of course, he already got the message from her."

"I was smiling . . ."

"She was looking . . ."

"You already knew . . ." Dr. Sachs is playacting: " 'Yes, you're absolutely right. The kids are running around and raising lots of hell on the train.' . . . That's a very appropriate topic to talk about. A naturally occurring event that everyone is going to be interested in. Easy to talk about. Not threatening. Good choice. That's one."

"Gee, you can expect *anything* in these cars."

"That eye contact was good."

"How? In what way, Celeste?"

"He looked at me right in the eye, but very briefly so he didn't threaten me."

"What about the expression of affect in his facial muscles?"

"Well, he didn't seem relaxed, Doctor."

"I wasn't relaxed?"

"You were a little . . . stiff about it."

"He smiled, he smiled a lot. But it was kind of . . . stiff."

"Stiff?"

"Yeah, stiff. You maintained your smile the whole time you said, 'Boy, anything can happen on these trains,' but you kind of froze. You expressed the feeling in your face, and that's good; but you should put the facial expression in your face and then pull it away. It's like the eye contact: you look, make eye contact, and then pull away. Okay? That's two. Let's hear the third."

"Sure can't concentrate on my newspaper with these kids making all that racket!"

"How was that?"

"Your smile was better."

"What made it better?"

"It was just a half-smile."

"And the eye contact?"

"Excellent. You looked at me, then you looked at the kids, and then you looked back at me. That was very relaxed. But your mouth was a little . . . stiff."

"How did he come across, speechwise?"

"Fine. It was like, you're not depending on me for something. You're just saying that to yourself, and you're including me."

"Okay. You add one line from now on, Celeste, so he can respond to that. Number four."

There is a long silence. Then Dr. Sachs bangs several times on the table and explains, "A lot of clutter noise, kids making noise."

Jim laughs. "I'm running out!"

"You can't run out. All you have to do is say the same thing you said before."

Jim laughs nervously. "It's impossible."

"Don't reinvent the wheel! Use it again and again. We won't tell." Friendly laughter from Dr. Sachs.

"These kids are sure making a lot of noise."

"Yes, they are, I can't stand it."

"I can't wait until I get to my stop."

"That was very natural. It flowed. He's very good. The smile wasn't as successful, though. Smiling relaxed me. Made me feel comfortable."

"The more facial expression you give to others, the more comfortable you feel. And they feel. So they're going to respond to you. You didn't avoid her, though. You looked at her."

"You turned to me a little bit, but not too much."

"You didn't put her on the spot. If you wanted to put some pressure on her, you'd put the eye contact right on her, and hold."

"Then I wouldn't even want to answer it."

"Holding your body position towards her also puts a lot of pressure on her. Whereas if you move back and forth while saying, 'Boy, they're making a lot of noise,' it's like spraying the lawn—talk, eye contact, away, back, it's not a fixed hold, so she doesn't have to feel that she's got to respond. The important thing is that it's moving back and forth in a very relaxed way. In the beginning you were jerking it back and forth. So why don't we just focus on that particular issue, this kind of spraying, giving some, taking away, moving in and out as you say the comment . . . Next. What number is it? Four or five?

Jim acts assertive. "A lot of noise . . ."

"Yeah, sure is, I can't stand it."

Jim is silent a while. "I don't know what to say next."

"That's all right. You don't have to say something every time. You can just pause. Let it go for a bit. And spray it a little."

"If you spoke to me on the El and I didn't know you, I might just say, 'Yes,' and not answer you that second. But I might still be interested, just waiting to see what you're going to say."

"In real conversations, it's not: you say something, I say something; you say something, I say something. It doesn't work that way. Sometimes what you say doesn't go anywhere. It doesn't mean that the person isn't interested; it doesn't mean that you should fold up your cards and leave; it just means you should ask again. Now, if repeatedly you get no response, well then, it means stop talking to her. But once doesn't mean that at all. Okay? Celeste, how was his facial expression?"

"You didn't smile."

"I was just thinking that maybe a smile wasn't as appropriate for that comment."

"No, it wasn't. So that was good. Even when you look at me and you look away, that makes me more interested. Also it was slower."

Jim is elated. "Yes, I did slow it down a little bit."

"You don't have to speak rapidly. There's no reason to. The more rapidly you speak, the less people listen to you." The doctor speaks slowly, articulating: "When you slow your speech down a little, it also conveys that you're more relaxed."

"How was your anxiety going?"

"Not too high."

"How was it when we started? What was it, from zero to 10?"

"Maybe . . . 6."

"How about now?"

"Two."

"Practice decreases anxiety. What do you think holds you back from going ahead and talking, Jim? Is it your laryngeal muscles that are tight, interfering with . . ."

"It's not the stutter, because I-I rarely st-stutter on the f-first comment. Um . . . I'm not sh-sure. When I do stutter, I clench my hands a little b-bit, my facial m-muscles, my neck, I kind of hunch my sh-shoulders . . ."

"Okay. Today we talked, primarily, about facial expression again, but we spent a lot of the time on the concept of 'spray,' or amount of contact with the person you're talking with. How to kind of dip in and out; how to dip into the conversation, then dip out. Move in, move out. Get involved, out. Mix them because that makes the person you're talking with most comfortable. And the more comfortable she is talking with you, the more comfortable you're going to be talking with her. Well, you have the skill. It's right there. It's right there. Practice."

6
Rate

e are listening to a tape of
a "feedback session." The patient has made a tape of his
masturbation fantasy, and the doctor and patient review
passages together and comment on them. The patient's
twice-recorded voice sounds toneless and mechanical.

"We-are-lying-together-in-bed-and-we-are-really-
enjoying-each-other's-company. Now-we-are-in-bed-
together-and-we-are-running-our-hands-over-each-
other's-bodies . . . lying-side-by-side . . . running-my-
hands-over-her-breasts . . . running-my-fingertips-
gently-over-her-nipples-and-her-breasts. Sliding-my-

hands-down-over-her-sides . . . over-her-thighs . . .
her-vagina. It's-really-turning-me-on . . ."

*Sounds good. [He fast-forwards tape.] Who do you
imagine?*

It was just someone that I had seen the other day.

*It's important to use people that you actually see,
people in the real world. There's no sense in developing
arousal to someone you'll never have contact with. No
sense in getting aroused to Marilyn Monroe, because
she's dead. You have to become aroused to people in
your natural environment, people that you can poten-
tially access.* Playboy *bunnies only exist thanks to air-
brushes in Chicago.*

"What's happening here?" I ask Dr. Sachs. "What are we
listening to?"

"This is a tape recording of a therapy session during
which I play back the tapes that the patient has developed
while masturbating. We actually tape-record these sessions to check on whether he's done it or not."

"You tape-record it yourself? So you're in the room?"

"Oh, no, we're not in the room. He does this at home.
He brings the tapes in and I critique them."

"But he has to verbalize it."

"He has to verbalize it out loud, because we don't trust
sexual deviates."

"You don't trust the patient, but you trust his verbalization."

"Well, it's a little closer to reality. If a person comes
with a tape that's filled with an hour of deviant material,
I know that the individual has used deviant material for
one hour. I know that . . . So now you're going to listen to
me spot-checking three hours of masturbatory satiation.
The patient is a thirty-five-year-old caucasian male, re-

ferred here six months ago following his arrest for his one and only conviction of a sexual crime, which was the rape of a young woman. He was found guilty, but placed on probation. He has completed sixty masturbatory sessions and also had some additional desensitization for a problem with a facial tic. And he's undergone assertiveness and social skill training—fifteen sessions."

"The tape recording includes both his tapes and your comments?"

"Yes. So there are two tape recorders sitting in the office during the feedback session. One is playing the patient's tape intermittently, the other is recording the conversation he and I are having about that tape."

"So that mechanical voice we heard in the background is the recording of his own recording."

"That's right. It's the tape in which he describes out loud the fantasies he masturbates to, while actually doing it."

"We-are-lying-together-in-bed. I-feel-the-warmth-of-her-body-beneath me. I-really-care-about-you, I-really-care-about-how-you-feel. I-love-to-be-with-you. As-we-are . . ."

You really care about her. That's quite acceptable. That would be true of anyone you're dating. Why would you date someone you didn't want to be with?

". . . how-you-feel-about-me. I-can-feel-the-warmth-of-your-body-beneath-me . . ."

That was kind of carrying out a little dialogue?
I was trying to.
That's okay. Or you could say, "I tell her, 'I really enjoy being with you.' " She doesn't have to say, "And I love you now and forever." That would be inappropriate. Uh . . .

"I-feel-my-penis-sliding-into-her-vagina. That-really-feels-exciting-to-me. I-feel-the-warmth-of-her-vagina-around-my-penis . . ."

How would you know that she's enjoying it?
Only if she says so.
That would be one way. Or by her initiation. You can add, "And she really wants to have the sensation of my penis in her vagina. She really enjoys feeling me thrusting. She's really taking charge because she's turned on." So there's a clear message from her behavior and plenty of thought as to what she wants. It's exciting to you, but it's really exciting to her. You understand?
Uh huh.
It is characteristic of people having sex that they are exquisitely timid. And I'll tell you why. It's because there never was a course in school that you took, like math, a course dealing with how to communicate to your lover about what kind of sexual activity you would like him or her to perform. When couples get together, they kind of act like they see in the movies. They hope that this is the right thing, instead of talking about what it is that they enjoy. So when you get involved with someone, it is exceedingly helpful for you to be direct and to ask your partner what he or she likes.

"It-really-feels-good-to-have-her-hands-on-my-penis . . . to-have-my-penis-in-her-vagina . . ."

That's good, that she's doing the guiding. There's no question about it, about her cooperation.

"When a patient elaborates with you on normal fantasies, do you have him write them down?"
"Oh, no. I want him to be able to generate them on his own."

"But don't you make up the material?"

"No, I don't make up the material."

"Didn't I hear you dictate something to him?"

"Oh, I just gave him tips for things to add. Many times the patients don't know how to use these fantasies, fantasies they used to be aroused to. Of course, some never were . . ."

"And you get them turned on to the normal fantasy."

"*I* don't get them turned on to it, *they* get turned on to it. I don't demand that they use it every time. I wouldn't want them to do that. And I keep it short. By definition, it's got to be short. I don't want them to ruminate about it. Repeated use of the same kind of cues would destroy the spontaneity."

I started to fantasize about more activities than I had before, and that raised the level of arousal.

What kind of activities did you include?

Oral sex.

That's good. You need to expand your repertoire.

". . . with-you. I-like-it, it-really-turns-me-on. It-turns-me-on-that-you-like-to-have-oral . . ."

Now, in reality, when you're making love to a woman, you wouldn't say, "I really like oral sex." You would say, "I really like to lick you." You see? It's a little less formal.

"I'm-turning-her-on-when-I-am-licking-her-vagina . . ."

Excellent. Now, what are you doing with your hands? Where would they be?

Probably on her upper legs, her thighs.

Uh huh. Or you could be feeling her torso, feeling her breasts, feeling her ass. Make it as real as possible, and as clear as possible. So you can plan those thoughts and *those ideas and think about them. Because the more you think about them, the easier they become in the future.*

"You encourage him to go deeper into these 'normal' attractions, then."

"If that's his desire, we help him reach that goal."

"Why didn't he have this desire to start with?"

"His desire is to not be arrested. Or his desire is not to have his marriage fall apart. Or his desire is not to have his picture on the front page of the newspaper as a child molester. And many of them had that happen to them, so they want to dodge that."

"I'm-touching-her-nipples. I'm-running-my-hand-over-her-nipples . . . She-has-her . . . [voice falters] hands-on-my-head, stroking-my-head . . ."

You could say, "I feel the warmth of her body, a warm sensation . . ."

"I'm-getting-really-turned-on. She's-driving-me-to-her-vagina . . . It-turns-me-on . . . Makes-me-close-to-her. Feeling-the-warmth-of-her-body . . ."

Excellent. You really enjoyed that experience.

"You have a way to assess positive reaction to the new erotic models?"

"We measure the basic arousal to deviant and nondeviant thoughts every time we evaluate them. Some of these individuals lose their arousal. Some don't lose it, but learn to control it. And some don't lose it and don't control it."

"So, ideally, what would you like to happen?"

"I would like to help them gain control over their behavior so that they don't go back to jail."

"It-feels-good-to-be-inside-of-her-because-she-wants-me-to . . . [the doctor fast-forwards] . . . angry. It-will-be-nice-to-have-a-deviant-fantasy . . . just-for-once."

Excellent.

"I-enjoy-seeing-her-body . . . grabbing-her-body-without-her-wanting-me-to. I-am-pulling-off-her-shirt. I-see-her-breasts. Now-she's-fighting-me-because-I'm-pulling-off-her-dress. She's-trying-to-stop-me-but-I'm-going-to-pull-them-off . . ."

This is a description of a rape?
Uh huh.
While you're describing it, you imagine the particular woman that you actually raped?
Yeah.

"Now-I-see-her-naked-before-me. She's-scared-and-angry. But-there's-nothing-she-can-do-about-it. I'm-going-to-stick-my-penis-in-her-vagina. I'm-going-to-stick-my-penis-in-her-vagina . . ."

You repeat that because it's particularly erotic to you?
Yeah.
Good.

"She's-telling-me-to-stop-but-I-won't-stop-until-I'm-finished . . ."

Did you ever worry that using these fantasies might increase your arousal?
Yeah. Or else that it might cause them to remain the same.
Well, I would anticipate that, initially, you might have gotten more turned on, because you probably avoided using them like the plague since your arrest. And then when you start using them again, you have

that rush back to, "Hey, that's really exciting." And then, for a short time, it might actually increase your arousal. But that only occurs if you're using these fantasies to ejaculate as rapidly as possible, then stopping. But you're not using them that way any more. You've started using them during boredom, then during the aversion, then during extremely aversive sessions. They can't maintain that much. They just can't.

"I'm-forcing-my-penis-in-her-vagina . . ."

Is this a young girl or an adult?
Young girl.
Young girl, okay.

"She-really-hates-it. It-is-upsetting-her, but-I-don't-care. I-still-continue-to-rape-her. I'm-forcing-my-penis-into-her-vagina. It-really-feels-good-and-I'm-really-getting-excited. I'm-really-hurting-her. I'm-forcing-my-penis-into-Janine's-vagina. I'm-raping-her. I'm-raping-Janine."

You should put more references to her age into it. And also what she looks like—the girl's appearance, her body. That's part of the thing that turned you on. How old is she? Twelve?
Yes.
How do you imagine her looking?
Just starting to develop, with small breasts, quite slender, thin, very young, smooth skin.
So you'll describe her like this: "I'm raping this twelve-year-old girl. She has a young body. She has almost no breasts. She has no hips. Her body isn't filled out. I'm raping this young girl who looks like . . ." You see? It's not just, "I'm raping a twelve-year-old-girl," but, "I'm raping a twelve-year-old girl whose body

*looks like—whatever it looks like—and whose breasts
are like . . . and whose legs are like . . . and whose buttocks are like . . ." So that it starts you thinking about
exactly the things that seemed to be erotic. How erotic
is it now?*

*Well, not nearly as much as it was, and not nearly as
much as the nondeviant.*

*If 10 is supererotic, and zero not erotic at all, where
would you put adult women?*

Three.

And where would you put young boys?

Zero.

*And where would you put young girls? Age twelve or
less?*

Ten.

*Okay. But be sure to include the physical character-
istics of the girl's body. If it's the youngness of her
breasts, the youngness of her hips, that are part of your
arousal, then that's what you've got to kill off.*

". . . fantasize-that-I'm-raping-a-young-girl . . . a-
young-girl-about-twelve-years-old. I'm-just-going-to-
rape-her . . . not-caring-about-what-she-thinks. I'm-
just-going-to-rape-her-and-satisfy-my-own-needs. I-
really-fool-myself. I-think-I'm-not-really-hurting-her.
I'm-not-doing-anything-wrong. She's-just-having-fun-I-
tell-myself. I-rape-this-twelve-year-old-girl. I-really-
hurt-her. I'm-forcing-her-to-take-her-clothes-off . . ."

*One thing we haven't talked about is how to incor-
porate more of the getting this young girl to the place
where you would force yourself on her. You see, even if
it's not part of the actual rape, it's still part of what led
you to getting in trouble. So you want to destroy it as
much as possible. That's what you've got to do. Incorporate some of the traps, expand more on the anteced-*

ents to getting to the girl, so it's really boring. You'll say, "I'm sitting in my car, waiting until a young girl goes by so I can rape her. I'll get her over to my car somehow, and I'm sitting in my car and I'm waiting until she comes." You're following me? It's important, because if you destroy these thoughts and urges, then what follows isn't going to follow. You need to treat these as if they were also part of your arousal pattern. So you're going to include them in there and bore yourself to death.

"I'm-assaulting-her-most-private-parts-because-that-excites-me. She's-telling-me-to-stop-so-I-make-her-spread-her-legs-even-wider-for-me. She-does-not-like-it-at-all . . ."

She doesn't like it.

"She-hates-being-raped. She-does-not-like-me, I-do-not-like-her. There-is-no-tenderness-between-us . . ."

What do you mean, you "do not like her"?
I couldn't like her if I'm raping her, I guess.

"I'm-grabbing-Janine's-ass. I'm-really-getting-turned-on . . . really-excited. She-hates-me-for-raping-her. She's-really-scared-of-me. She-doesn't-know-what-I'm-going-to-do-next. I-like-to-dominate-her-and-be-in-control . . ."

Are those your own words, David—"dominate and control"?
Well, they come easily into my mind.
Maybe that's exactly how you feel. I'm just wondering. Is that a product of your therapy in the past or is that how you've always felt?
It's part of what I always felt.

I just wanted to make sure. If they're the words that you use and the thoughts that you think, then keep them in. It's good, though. You're coming along well.

Sometimes it bothers me that I don't ejaculate during the nondeviant part.

How does it bother you?

That I'm not getting excited enough to it.

In the past, you've used thoughts of rape to generate more arousal . . .

Almost always, yes.

In so doing, you allowed the nonaggressive sexual fantasies to drop to the side. So what happened is that the nonaggressive ones got less erotic to you. You said, "Gee, I need more excitement, I'll use the aggressive," and so you drifted into using more aggressive thoughts. Well, your treatment has to really do two things. It has to eliminate your arousal to the aggressive, but it also has to maintain or expand your arousal to the nonaggressive part. Nonaggressive elements are new to you. Caring, concern about who you're having sex with, that's new. So you shouldn't expect it, initially, to be as erotic. You shouldn't expect that. You've been using aggressive thoughts a long time. It's going to take you a while to get away from them.

I haven't had any sexual experiences of the loving type, so I don't have any memories to draw on.

It's probably strange and unusual for you.

I'm not used to it. If I saw a girl walking down the street, I would think more of the deviant type of thought.

Grabbing her and raping her?

[Silence.]

Anal sex?

Yeah.

With some degree of pain on her part?

Not necessarily.
Uh huh.

"And-now-I-will-make-this-woman-suck-my-penis.
She's-begging-me-not-to, she's-trying-to-get-away.
But-I'm-holding-her-down. I'm-forcing-my-penis-into-
the-mouth-of-this-woman-who-I-am-raping. I'm-
forcing . . ."

It's a lot like forcing anal intercourse on her, forcing
oral sex on her. That turns you on a lot, or has turned
you on a lot. That's exactly what you need to put into
these fantasies. And, by the same token, you can also
take the anal intercourse and put that into a nondeviant
fantasy of anal sex with a woman when she wants to
have anal sex.
Can that be nondeviant?
Absolutely. One of my patients knows this woman—
he was painting her house—who described her sexual
activities to him. She really enjoyed having anal sex.
He would lay her down, touch her body, massage her
with lotion, and then have anal intercourse with her.
And that's what she really loved. As a matter of fact,
that was the best sexual experience that she had.
For some reason I don't feel comfortable about put-
ting it in a nondeviant fantasy. I've always thought of
it as being a little . . . kinky.
You've just developed some stereotypes—that good
girls don't do this, and only bad girls have this done to
them. It all depends on what you like and what she
would like. And matching up, so to speak.

"And-I-feel-my-penis-deep-in-her. She-wants-me-to-
stop, she's-telling-me-to-stop, but-I-won't-stop-until-
I'm-finished . . ."

That's what you want to do. You want to make it as
erotic as possible. [Sighs.] So let's do this twice a day.

Uh . . . when I masturbate so much, it's difficult for me to be aroused by any sexual thoughts.

That's true, but I wanted to make certain that you're in good control over your arousal, that your arousal was reduced. I certainly wouldn't want you to get involved with any rapes while you're here.

I was thinking about how, since I've come here, I've moved forward in some ways, and backward too.

In what ways?

Well, forward, because right now I really don't have any urge—at all—to rape or to expose myself. These are the two fantasies I've done on tape so far. And backward in the sense that I feel less remorse for the victim than I did before I came here. Maybe because we haven't discussed that as I did a lot with psychologists before. It really hasn't been on my mind at all here.

I guess that's true. We haven't spoken about it. Well, one of the things I want you to do is not have thoughts in the first place. If you don't have any thoughts, you don't have any urges. But it sounds like doing two sessions a day is going to really knock down your arousal, though. Is that too much?

Yeah.

We'll reduce it to one session a day.

That's good enough. It would bore me more with the deviant, but then I can't get very excited about the nondeviant.

You don't want that. You want the deviant to be boring . . . It's a long hour, isn't it? We're about half-way into it.

"What if patients don't have an orgasm?"

"If they don't, they don't. We can't force someone to have an orgasm. But if they do have an orgasm, and keep masturbating, that's good. They will associate the post-

orgasmic letdown with the deviant sexual act. Most do
have an orgasm within the first few minutes, then continue for the whole hour. That's the key thing, doing the
whole hour. Repeating over and over. Ejaculation is not
the point. I teach them to slow down, to bore themselves,
to extinguish a particular element of the fantasy until it
becomes really aversive. Then I tell them to move on to
the next element."

"Still masturbating?"

"Oh sure, attempting to masturbate."

> *I'm going to change the victim a little while later.*
> *Why?*
> *Because it was more erotic.*
> *Who did you change the victim to?*
> *The girl next door.*
> *Oh, that same girl?*
> *Yes.*
> *Let's listen to it.*

"The-girl-is-just-about-to-walk-by-now-and-I'm-
hiding. I'm-hiding-in-the-alley. She's-just-about-ready-
to-walk-by-now. I-want-to-show-her-my-penis. My-big-
penis. I-want-to-show-my-penis-to-this-young-girl-
because-I-want-to-surprise-her . . . shock-her. I-want-
to-show-her-my-penis-because-it-excites-me . . ."

> *David, is this the first tape in which you used the*
> *exposure?*
> *Yes.*
> *Have you ever exposed yourself to that girl?*
> *No. Because then everyone would know.*
> *Did you feel that you would get away with the rape?*
> *Uh . . . yes, I did.*
> *Why don't you include that in one of your rape fan-*
> *tasies: "And I know no one is going to find me out after*

I've raped her"? Because it's those kinds of beliefs that you want to destroy.

"She's-really-scared-this-young-girl. She-doesn't-like-me-showing-her-my-penis. She-looks-disgusted-this-young-girl-who-I'm-showing-my-penis-to . . ."

It's good that you put those qualifiers in. You keep making it very clear what's going on.

"Is that the same patient?"
"Yes. During the course of the interview, it turned out that the most serious problem was his lifelong pedophilia, which is his arousal to young kids. He's primarily a pedophilic exhibitionist, that is, he exposed himself to young girls. He's never been arrested for that, although he's been doing it for years. He also hands out pornography or leaves it on the sidewalk for the young girls to pick up and watches them as they look at it."

How do you imagine her face?
A combination of being surprised and a kind of disgust.
Disgust about what?
I guess about seeing someone expose himself.

". . . I'm-really-excited-to-show-her-my-penis. I'm-not-thinking-about-how-this-will-affect-her."

You purposely try and not think about what's in her head?
Well, no. That just wouldn't enter my mind while I'm doing it.
What do you think she thinks?
She can't understand why anybody would want to expose themselves. She probably thinks, "Here's this weird man."

You want the kid to wonder why you're doing this?
Um . . . no.
You want her to think that you're weird?
Um . . . not necessarily that either.

"This-young-girl-is-trying-to-run-away-because-she's-scared . . . and-shocked. She-looks-disgusted-by-it . . ."

That's pretty erotic to you, that she's running away?
Uh . . . no.
What's the most exciting part about exposing yourself to little girls?
Um . . . the moment when they just see my penis.
Why is that so erotic?
I guess because I think of them seeing it as being nasty and dirty. The thought arouses me. That, and the act of exposing.
You could say, "I'm holding my penis right there in my hands. I look down and I see my erect penis. I'm holding my erect penis and these young girls are looking right over. Right now they see my erect penis. They're looking right at my penis. I see their faces the very moment that they see my erect penis." Make it as real as possible.

". . . doesn't-understand-why-I'm-showing-her-my-penis. It-makes-the-thirteen-year-old-girl-scared-of-me. She-is-looking-at-my-penis-in-shock. She-doesn't-want-to-look-at-my-penis-because-it-is-nasty-and-dirty . . ."

Nasty and dirty—that seems to come in. Anal sex, exposing yourself, your penis . . . Is sex nasty and dirty for you?
Not if it was with someone who wanted to.
Let's say masturbating. Is that nasty and dirty?
Yes.
Ninety-nine percent of males and 65 percent of fe-

males masturbate. So what you're saying is that 99 percent of all males participate in nasty, dirty things?

What about the 1 percent that don't?

They are really bizarre, I think. Very peculiar folks. That really requires a screwed-up head. Why do you think the issue of dirty is such a turn-on for you? Any idea?

Maybe because sex is never talked about in our family.

Well, that's a clear message, isn't it? It's like saying that it's bad. You've got kind of a normal family then . . . How do you feel, what impact does it have, me listening to these tapes?

At first I didn't like the idea too much, but now it doesn't really matter. Doesn't upset me much any more.

Good.

"I-enjoy-having-them-see-my-penis. But-they-do-not-like-it-so-they-are-running-away. They-are-scared-because-I-showed-them-my-penis . . ."

There's that "being scared" again. It seems to come up a lot . . .

I might not actually fantasize about them being scared. I'm trying to plant seeds of reality into my head.

7
Bore

"When you listened to the tapes, you heard a lot of positive statements from me. It's not that the patient is doing so many positive things, I simply want him to feel that he can do the therapy."

"Your patients need a lot of encouragement?"

"Oh, sure. The individual is faced with the dilemma that he is aroused to something that's highly erotic, that he's enjoyed for years, that he thoroughly loves, and then he has to do this therapy which is boring, uninteresting, and eventually aversive, which is ridding him of the things that he loves, cherishes, and desires. So his dilemma is: Shall I do the therapy?"

"You want him to want it."

"Every therapist needs the patient to cooperate. You don't have to listen to the tapes to figure out if he does. If he doesn't, there just are no tapes!"

"In a sense, then, the treatment consists of giving him everything he wants."

"We certainly try to get him to use the best possible and most deviant sexual fantasy he's ever had. If it's a rapist, I specially want him to use the most aggressive rape possible: lack of concern for the victim, using her as an object . . ."

"You really go out of your way to satisfy your customers."

"Yeah, we *satiate* them. Think 'extinction.' "

"What is it called?"

"Masturbatory satiation. It's the most fascinating way we found of destroying deviant arousal. Satiation, extinction."

"You have them masturbate to death."

"Right. You've got it: postorgasm. Let's say you're talking about some married fellow. You want him to develop an extremely boring sexual life. Well, you don't *want* him to, but let's pretend. What you would do is simply have him have sex in the same way, at the same time, with the same woman, with the same kind of experiences, in the same position. Always. For a couple of years."

"That's *nondeviant* sex . . ."

"Yeah, that's right. And that will be extremely boring for the individual. Now let's say that you're dealing with a child molester who's aroused by children, and you want to destroy those thoughts and urges. What do you do? Well, you take the part that's deviant and highly erotic and you go over it again and again, so many times, until it's *really boring*."

"It has the simplicity of great discoveries."

"Thank you."

"Boredom therapy. All the sex you can get."

"And more."

"I'm impressed."

"Thank you."

"Some positive destruction you're doing there. A Copernican revolution."

"Positive destruction? What's that?"

"Well, you don't take a knife and cut the deviant part out, do you?"

"Let me tell you, I don't care what it's called!"

"I meant, you don't try to suppress it, like in the old days."

"Oh, heavens no."

"You keep dumping his own product on the patient. 'Suck it in and spit it out!' It's the epitome of consumerism."

"Actually, I would hope that I use a therapy that's very close to a naturally occurring phenomenon. The reason I approve of it is because it's logically sound. Secondly, it's easier for the patients to do. When we develop a therapy that is so divergent from what is normally done, it's hard to point out to them how to do the therapy, and hard to explain why it's effective. Whereas if you select a therapy that is very close to the real world, it's much easier for the patients to do."

"What's the origin of this therapy?"

"Historically, the man who started all this was Kurt Freund. He made his initial studies in Czechoslovakia at the end of the fifties. Now he's in Toronto."

"That's amazing. The technique originated in Europe. And from a Communist country!"

"That's right. Freund was commissioned to differentiate between homosexual and heterosexual men who were in the army. At that time homosexuality was considered to be pretty abnormal. Freund quickly moved to presenting slides of young children to establish not only sex preferences, but also age preferences. And it was Gene Abel, down in Georgia, who expanded the technique to most deviant sexual interests by putting everything on audiotapes. His clinic has been operating for years, and he's certainly done more research than anyone else has done, or is likely to do, for a long time in the business."

"So at the beginning the technique wasn't specially meant for sexual deviates?"

"No. Bill Marshall first used it kind of in reverse, to treat sexual dysfunctions."

"Masturbatory satiation is actually a spin-off of orgasm therapy?"

"If you like, yes. The successful part of the early work with masturbatory satiation wasn't satiation. It was, instead, masturbatory conditioning to *increase* arousal. Bill Marshall's real contribution is that he took it and applied it to deviant sexuality and lengthened the amount of time for the satiation procedure. Masturbatory conditioning was used on a normative basis in individuals who were bisexuals and were aroused by males, or women aroused by females, and found it conflictual. Marshall managed to satiate the other element they were aroused by. He was able to inhibit it by looping, which makes it boring."

"Canada seems to have been very active in that kind of research."

"It's been in the forefront, if you look at it in terms of population. There are more programs in the United States, but there seem to be more people doing evaluative research and pioneering work in Canada."

"How do you explain that? Are there more sexual deviates in Canada?"

"No, I don't think so. It's just easier to set up programs there. The political and ethical climate within the Canadian system is a lot less stringent than here—patients' rights and all that."

"Is the same technique used in other areas of treatment?"

"Phobias. I just treated a mouse-phobic. I had the lady buy ten mice and bring them into therapy. She was frightened to death, of course. She would hold my hand while I lifted them by the tail. Then she touched the tail too and realized it wasn't weird at all."

"Of mice and women."

"She practiced at home, picking one up and putting it back in the box."

"Did she really have to go through that? I wouldn't do it myself."

"She had a house in the mountains and she couldn't live there because of the mice."

"So you put her back in her box. I read about an agoraphobic housewife who had locked herself up in her room. After intensive behavioral therapy, she conquered her fears. She finally managed to make it—to the supermarket."

"Agoraphobics fear losing control. They frighten themselves over what will happen in the future. More often than not, nothing happens."

"This would frighten me even more. Now, holding a housewife by the hand or a rat by the tail is one thing . . ."

"Not a rat; a mouse."

"A mouse, or a man . . . but to shift an arousal around is another story."

"Friendly mice or fearful mice, it's just the movement from one to the other, is it not? Arousal to young girls versus arousal to adult women—it's just another shift."

"Yes, but the only thing you hold on to, in that case, is fantasies."

"We treat phobic symptoms in fantasy too. That's called

systematic desensitization. In fact, I just finished the treatment of a fellow who was fearful of losing his erection. At thirty-five he had never managed to get it up with a woman. I developed a series of fearful situations for him, all the images that caused him not to get an erection, or to lose it. I taught him how to imagine these scenes when he's completely relaxed, and pretty soon he started relating. It took him forty sessions."

"It may have gone faster if the rat-lady had practiced on him . . . By the way, though, desensitization actually destroys the anxiety, not the arousal. Is satiation reserved to sex offenders?"

"No, no. They've treated individuals who like to hoard towels in psychiatric hospitals. The treatment involves giving them more towels, overloading them, satiating them with towels, till the whole room is filled with them. Then they give up. It's the same principle."

"Don't you find that a little sad?"

"What?"

"After all, what else is there to *do* in a psychiatric hospital, except hoard things?"

"Well . . ."

"Masturbate, I suppose. And fantasize about towels."

"Wait a minute. The fellows I'm dealing with don't fantasize about towels. They've been using deviant fantasies a long time, for ten years. They've molested thirty kids."

"In their heads?"

"No, in reality."

"And satiating fantasies takes care of the behavior?"

"Absolutely. That's why we do it. You see, sex is not in the body, it's in the head. What's erotic is what you think of. Mostly, it's your interpretation of what's going on. Next time you have sex, close your eyes and don't think about who is with you."

"That happens."

"It's not half as enjoyable."

"Behavior and thought are two different things. In psychoanalytic terms, a fantasy is a mental phenomenon. It doesn't specifically have to do with behavior."

"I don't know if it's critical to make the distinction. From a treatment point of view, I find the person with the thoughts almost as dangerous as the person with the behavior."

"But fantasies may simply compensate for sexual frustrations. Would you track down fantasies that an individual has never acted upon?"

"First of all, I don't have to track them down anymore. The patient tracks them down himself during masturbation. I just sit and listen. And just because the individual hasn't acted upon his fantasies, doesn't mean much to me. They still have power over his life."

"That's quite a big jump, don't you think?"

"Yeah. If you don't want to take the jump, don't jump. But if you change the behavior, and not the fantasy, they'll recommit the crime."

"Don't you end up punishing the individual twice?"

"Listen, until you have interviewed twenty rape victims, I'd suggest you step cautiously in this area. Rape is something very devastating."

"No question about it. But what if someone fantasized a rape in a consensual relation? Would you also object to that? After all, you encouraged the ass-man to keep feeling his women . . ."

"That's too fine a line for me to walk. You have to consider the potential victim. There are some people who find the description of the rape of a woman more exciting the more the woman resists. And that's a very serious indication. That means that they need the violent aspect to get excited."

"Would you say that arousal to rape is present in everyone, especially in males?"

"Some studies have shown that it depends on how you

present the rape of a woman. You can change the sexual arousal by changing the woman's reaction. You can set up a situation in which a woman will fight and find the whole business abhorrent. You can also sketch another situation —this is Hollywood—where the man starts raping the woman, she fights a little bit, and then, *in spite of herself*, becomes aroused and finally orgasms. Normal men will find that more exciting than the purely violent one. But that's not a research question that I'll ask. We don't care in what way you can make someone sexually aroused. I'm more interested for the moment in the precision of discrimination we can get between rapists and nonrapists."

"Then you could actually *increase* the arousal to violence in normal men?"

"No. That would raise highly ethical problems."

"But it would be feasible?"

"Yes, we could do that, logically speaking. But that's not something I would try."

"What's behind this idea of satiation?"

"The theory behind satiation is that there is a constant ratio in a person between the frequency of occurrence of deviant and nondeviant sexual thought, and that deviant urges result from altering that ratio. In my protocol case, by overwhelming the individual with the deviant . . ."

A phone rings in the next room. "We have a hot line for people to call in with various deviations," Dr. Sachs briefly explains.

"I think you're right. Satiation sounds very boring."

"If you look at this graph, boredom is the broken line, the solid line is the deviant fantasy, and zero is the beginning of the treatment. You'll note, as time goes on, the boredom getting more and more boring."

"I agree. It's definitely boring."

"That's greater displeasure in this direction. See it moving up . . . up . . . up? Now it's peaked out there for the deviant!"

"Congratulations!"

"Thank you."

"Do you ever get aroused by your patients' fantasies? Do you discover through them something about your own sexuality?"

"About *my* sexuality?"

"You're exposed to a lot of fantasies . . ."

"Oh yes. Quite frankly, I think it has a satiation effect on me. I've been a sex researcher for ten years, and sometimes I get fed up with it, you know. I talk with people about sex *all day long*, and it does get to be a drag."

"You never find some of their fantasies particularly appealing?"

"Well, I'm not attracted to young girls, so it's not particularly erotic to me. Secondly, I'm too busy doing the treatment, trying to help the patient generate more exciting fantasies *for him*, to get turned on to them myself. I saw last night this individual who is into spanking young boys. That's what he gets off on, you remember. Now, I'm not sitting there listening to his fantasy hoping that I'll get titillated. What I'm doing is describing how to make his fantasy even *more* erotic, so that a greater repetition occurs. Because he's in a very dangerous situation there, spanking young boys."

"You find boredom powerful?"

"Can you find me something stronger?"

"In sexual terms?"

"That's what I said. Find me something stronger."

"It's stronger than electric aversion?"

"That's correct."

"Don't you think this is true for the culture as a whole?"

"I don't think so. The culture is constantly developing

new sexual things. That's why *Playboy* always has a different playmate every month."

"You read *Playboy?*"

"No, jeez! [Laughs.] When we have new technicians working in the lab, they're glued to the video. They want to see all the sexual activity. The second month they occasionally look at it. The third month they could care less. They get satiated pretty fast."

"Frankly, I suspect that certain aspects of speech have satiating properties that don't belong to the message per se. These properties could also be located in specific words or small phrases, or in their repetition."

"Repetition definitely plays a crucial role."

"But these properties can also be attributed to the 'performance' or 'delivery.' The tone may be dull, or the voice soporific. Then the problem is in determining when speech itself is the repetition of another property. If the speech is boring to start with, all the variants of the message will have the same satiating effect, by definition. We should distinguish the stereotypic features that are liable to generate a detumescence in the patient's arousal pattern, from purely linguistic features—which would be irrelevant to a discussion of satiation proper. As you well know, the same message may be used in different situations. A sex therapist explaining his treatment to a patient and a cardiologist interpreting an X-ray of the chest area may both declare, "This may lead to an arrest." Is the difference in situation sufficient to establish a difference in cardiac response? Linguists believe that *extra*linguistic factors will fall in a different zone of satiability. The exclusion from sexual satiation of the questions of performance and affect —that is, the pragmatics of boredom—is analogous to the division between linguistics proper and semantics. That view has limitations. For example, I doubt that it can readily account for such speech features as irony or humor."

"That's something I wouldn't want to philosophize about. I'm not attempting to satiate sexuality in general, I'm trying to bore the daylights out of a very narrow section of sex, the one which involves violence."

"But sexuality in general is also impulsive and excessive. It involves repulsion, fear, and irrationality. Why is it that all the metaphors of erotic literature associate sex with obscenity, sacrilege, aggression, war, death? If you eradicate all that, what's left?"

"There's plenty left."

"What?"

"The opportunity for closeness."

"Physical closeness?"

"Emotional closeness. That's what sex is about—a way of relating."

"Some kind of communication then?"

"Exactly. Most sexual problems come from a lack of communication. I teach people how to communicate what it is they want."

"Communication is far more encompassing than sexuality itself."

"I agree, but sexuality happens to be the locus of the symptom. It's the ticket. I like the idea of sex being less sexual than a built-in communication opportunity."

"Isn't sex, though, a very sensitive zone of communication for the individual?"

"The most sensitive."

"Yet you keep *desensitizing* it by making everything explicit. You even discuss with your patients in detail their own treatment."

"Oh, I tell them exactly what it is. There's no secret there."

"Precisely. Their sexuality is treated as something external to them, an adjunct, an object they're trained to look at from the outside."

"Right."

"Is there nothing private, or specific, or festive anymore about our sexuality?"

"Nothing. It's just one area of observable behavior, measurable by instruments. As we say in therapeutic language, we function on communication in the sexual area."

8
Reject

I got arrested about four years ago for a crime that involved someone younger than me. This was in Ohio. I was about seventeen. The person was fifteen, going on sixteen. There was just about one year difference between us, but that wasn't the point. The cops out there were after me all the time. They didn't particularly like me because I used to deal drugs, and they could never catch me at it. It was just marijuana, to make a few bucks. They'd stop me every time they could. It was that kind of city. You're constantly harassed whether you try to go straight or not.

And that's what happened. I had stopped dealing then,

133

but they busted me for sexual offense. They gave me the choice of either going to jail or leaving the country. So they deported me for that. I was a U.S. citizen at the time, too. But they did it anyway. I couldn't make any money in Spain because it's worse economically, so I came back into the country a year later and a neighbor informed on me. The police arrested me. I stayed in jail for two and a half months on $25,000 bail. They thought I was going to split if they let me out. They brought the old charge that they had on me, so I was put in solitary confinement. They gave me a five-year probation and I had to promise that I would go back and forth from Dayton to this clinic in Chicago. They would pay for an airline ticket.

I didn't know anything about the clinic. They were the ones that found it. It was part of my plea bargain. They make it look like it's voluntary, but half the people go to the clinic only because they sign a piece of paper. Have you been to the clinic? There's this guard at the door. You're not allowed to go in by yourself. You've got to wait downstairs so you don't get to the other floors and rape the personnel—that's why. You go every two weeks, and every time the probation officer knows you've been there. If you don't go, you're in trouble. They'd put you back in jail.

At the clinic they give you all these tests to fill out about what was wrong with you and how you feel about your problems. Of course I had to go along with it, all the quizzes and things to screen you, like, "I'm feeling a little girl's underpants," and how it arouses you, from 1 to 10. It didn't arouse me, but I did it anyway. How are you going to be truthful it they're going to lock you back up?

Oh, they had records on me, I'm sure they did. Records from the police. They knew I'd been arrested for public lewdness—that I had problems with that. I did that once. It's like a misdemeanor. I've had problems, but it wasn't strictly with kids, you know. They thought I was a pedophile, which isn't really true. You see, on my charges they put "having sex with a minor" and "endangering the welfare of a minor." But they don't put that we were only one year or two years apart, or whatever. They made it look as bad as they could, and now I have a felony on my record. One felony charge and a misdemeanor. It means I can't get a job as a cop. That would be my favorite thing, to be a big-city cop. But forget it now.

So anyway, they had a lot of tests at the clinic. They have so many that you get tired and fill them in without even reading them. You can only take so much. You get bored.

After that they give you this test where they connect this thing called a "penile transducer" and they let you watch this slide show. If you get an erection, it'll come out on the computer. They let you see these slides of adults, children, and a whole bunch of other things. Now if you get turned on to the picture of a kid, it'll stay in your mind because it's a dark, soundproof room. You'll still be turned on to it while they show you the next slide. They can't tell one from the other. The picture will go off in a couple of seconds, maybe three or four; you'll look at it, the computer will shut off, and another picture will come on. But if your erection isn't at the level you started with, it won't show you the next slide. It'll stop and wait for your erection to go down. And it's frustrating because it gets you horny and it stays in your mind. They'll have you do stuff like counting backwards from a hundred in threes to get whatever it is off your mind. It can take ten minutes sometimes. So it's very aggravating to sit there in the dark doing this counting over and over again dealing with getting erections . . .

You can't even touch yourself because it's a very sensitive machine, it'll set the whole computer off. It'll measure it as an erection if you breathe too hard. Any arm movement will trigger it, it's so delicate. You can stay there for two hours. So it's better if you don't have an erection. Because then, it'll keep on going and going without stopping.

I found out, instead of sitting there, waiting around two hours, that I could make it in twenty minutes. That's the thing.

A year later they put me on Depo-Provera. According to the tests, I needed it. This drug would stop you from getting an erection to *anything*. It's a female hormone, so it's going to reverse your sex drive to zero. That's to control you on the street. It was a funny thing. They said, "You can stop whenever you want." So I stopped, and they threatened to stop seeing me because I hadn't asked ahead of time. And if they had stopped seeing me, then the courts would have said, "Well, we gave him a chance and now he can go back to jail." So in order for me to pass the test, I would have to not be aroused at all. Then they gave me the test to make sure I was taking it. So I had to cheat the test. They have no way of telling. I'm on this side and the only glass where they can look in is where the projector goes through. The only thing they work with is your penis.

Now if you close your eyes or pinch yourself when you peak, to stop an erection from coming, they wouldn't know. They figure I'm on the drug and that's why I don't have an erection.

Not everyone is on the drug. They don't give you the medication just like that. This other guy was on it. He had no legs. He gets around in a wheelchair. He's a youth-group leader and he involved himself with boys, so he was taking a high dosage. I'm sure in a few years he's going to pay for that, for that amount of body at such a high dosage. And he kept taking it and taking it, because he believed these people. He's very moral and he hates what he did.

They got me to take it, and I went along with it because

of the courts. It made me look like I was doing the most I could. And once I got on it, it was impossible to get off. The doctor wouldn't let me quit. I was taking 100 milligrams a day for about two weeks. I had less sex drive, but I was getting sick.

So I just stopped. I went over to the clinic and told the doctor what I did, and he had a heart attack. He told me that I was the doctor, then, so I shouldn't even come and see him because I didn't listen to him. He said that if I did it one more time, he'd take me off the course. That's what he said. I've got witnesses. He said it in front of the group. And you know what taking me off would mean once the judge found out. So I stopped taking the drug, but I kept filling out these forms asking, "How many times did you get an erection today?" I just wrote, "low." I'd lie along to make it look like I was taking the drug. The court was paying for it, it's an expensive drug. I'd just flush it down the toilet to keep track in case they ever checked with the pharmacist. I kept on doing this until I got arrested about two months ago.

So you take tests for the first couple of weeks at the clinic. After that, you're put in a group. I was in a group of eight. The treatment started with people who like kids. Not all pedophiles—there were also rapists and masochists. They say these people can't get along in society. That's why they teach you these skills—"social skills" they call them. I don't think it was true for me, but that's okay. In Dayton I kept to myself because everyone knew about me. And I was on probation. I couldn't leave the house. I couldn't work. In Spain, I was more social. I was going to get married there before I came back. But I had to get up the money. In the little village of three hundred people where I stayed, there are no jobs. I could have lived in Madrid, but I don't like big cities.

You're in the group for three weeks. First of all, they

give you this book. It's a very good book. It tells you how to talk with people and how to introduce yourself to someone. Some people never go near adults. They're afraid because they have a low self-esteem. Reading what's in the book is supposed to help bring it up. Then everyone has a role model. You may pretend with someone in the group that you've just met them, or the doctor may pretend she's someone on the street and you're meeting her. Then, afterwards, people respond on how they feel about it. They give you feedback, and that's good. It works out *there*, although it's not so easy on the street, you know. It does give you will power, I guess.

You're supposed to improve after ten weeks. You're supposed to see the difference. I made a little bit of progress. I liked the whole thing. Some people didn't. They felt they were not going to socialize with people, anyway. They hardly talked to anyone in the clinic, even to us. They were quiet. That's how they are.

It helps people if they want it. If someone is a pedophile, it's not going to change your sex habits. Very few people are going to care for you if you're a pedophile. The only people you're going to be friends with are other pedophiles.

After the social-skill group, they start you out with what is called "masturbatory satiation" sessions. They give you an hour-long cassette and you're supposed to masturbate out loud for an hour, in your own home, in private. The doctor talks it over with you first. I did it. I took the tape home. It gets boring, like they say. I mean, when you're repeating the same thing over and over, like, "I'm exposing myself in front of a fifteen-year-old boy," and you're supposed to actually do twenty cassettes like that, it *is* boring.

So I did it, but I felt exactly the same. I didn't see any change at all. A lot of people came in and said it changed their ways, but they were all liars. They even told me on the side just to stop doing them.

I started with the masturbation, but after a few sessions I just talked into the tape recorder for an hour. Because it didn't do me any good. If it had done me anything, I would have enjoyed doing it. Even when I did masturbate for those ten sessions where I went through with it, it didn't do a damned thing. I still got off on the same stuff. I knew inside my head what turned me on. Everybody was telling me to cheat. Talk into the tape recorder and don't masturbate. So that's what I did. They don't know if you're masturbating. They just take your word. So I got a second tape recorder and played one and had the other record it. I'd be watching TV. When the hour was up, they'd both shut off and I'd bring the tape into the clinic.

Everyone does it. The doctors have it in their heads that it works. They could have made a lot of money as private psychiatrists, but they stayed there. They all want to be Sigmund Freud. Believe me, the invention doesn't work. After ten hours and ten tapes, nothing had happened. Nothing. You can only do something so long without being bored, you know. And I got other things to do.

I had to worry, also, about who would come into the room. My mother was wondering what I was doing in there with the door locked. I had to do it secretly, quietly. It's not something you go tell your parents about.

After ten weeks, they give you the test again. That's when people cheated. It's like a fight with the computer. Every little movement and it goes on and off. Some people close their eyes or stick a tack in their shoes and press on it to pinch their toes and stop the erection from coming. Some people would even steal the slides of the kids. [Laughs.] That's after they're supposed to be cured, and they're still after those porno things! You see, once I'm through going there, I'll be another "success" for them.

After a year, when the sessions are over, certain people are asked to stay because they don't feel as if they've been treated. Most people say they've been treated just to get out of here, but others will be honest. They get put in a group with this other doctor. That's when the drug comes into the picture. The guy is a psychiatrist, so he's a good talker. He'll talk you into the drug, into increasing the dosage more and more, like he did to me. The way he put it, you couldn't say no. There's no research data to support whether the drug does damage or not. People take the drug and hide the fact that they know they're never going to change.

I was the same after a year, so I continued, every two weeks. Then the drug started. The side effects were cold spells, sweating. They gave me two more drugs to stop those. I felt worse than before, so I threw them all out. I could never reach him. I just kept getting the message machine. Anyway I started pretending I was taking the drug. They would try to catch me off guard by making me take the test. I'd cheat and fake it and pass it.

There are a lot of people who aren't open at the clinic. The ones who aren't open are the worst, because they get depressed. They think there's something wrong with them. So they would go through the whole thing, thinking they could get help from it. There's that one guy I told you about who takes so much drug. He doesn't cheat on the tests. He's been in there two years now. He'll never change, and they know he hasn't changed either. He has this dream that he'll get back in with the kids, so he keeps at it. But there's no help. He's thirty-five. He went through all forty sessions and he's still there.

Another guy was involved with little girls. He did the clinic, and then, next thing you knew, the police were asking about him and then he was right back. In the clinic, it was: "Look at Lucas! Look how well he's done!" I talked to him on the phone, and to this day, after he's been through the whole clinic, the drugs and everything, he's still the same as day one.

The program can stop you temporarily, but once you're out, you're going to do it again. Because it's right there in your mind. It's something you develop as a child. But when you're twenty-two or thirty-five or sixty, forget it. You can't change it.

There's this other guy who admitted he was still having sex with minors, so he decided to move to New Mexico where the age of consent is only thirteen. The doctors agreed with him. They said that if he kept on in Chicago, he was just going to be arrested again.

On the other hand, I do think it helped rapists. They, at least, have sex with women. It just changes from violent to nonviolent. A lot of rapists talk down on themselves. They've been told that they're sick, that they should go to jail.

I had the same thing happen to me. You feel so bad, you start thinking of suicide. Convicted sex offenders have a high rate of suicide. I desperately wanted to change, that's why I wanted to go to the clinic. I tried to kill myself in jail. The pants I used to hang myself ripped. The judge felt sorry for me and he arranged for me to go to the clinic. I'm the only one in Dayton that ever went there.

Rapists say no girl would like them. They think they are ugly. So they become angry. The clinic teaches them how to get this anger out instead of taking it out on a woman. It helps them. That is, unless they rape little kids. That's something different. But with adult women, yes, it helps. They all said they didn't like to do it. They just had no control over it. They hated it after they had done it. They felt sorry for the girl and they wished it had never happened. But they enjoyed it while they did it.

I'm in favor of the clinic for them. I do think a rapist could go through the whole thing—get bored and quit his rape life. Social skills help them, it teaches them how to get dates.

There were only a few rapists when I was at the clinic

and only one that I know of now. The rest were pedophiles. I talked to the rapist guy a lot over the weeks. He says it helped him a great deal. But the rapists are the first ones to say they'll never do it again. A lot of people will lie to you. For all I know, he might be in jail now.

I don't think rape is normal, because you're hurting someone. If you're doing something where it's not consensual, it's wrong. My exposing myself is consensual, since I pay someone to let me do that. I don't just come out in broad daylight. I pick someone out. I tell them ahead of time. I did that in Dayton. But you couldn't get the same sex as you do here in the big city. I had a couple of girlfriends there, but they stopped seeing me when they read it in the paper. It ruins your whole life, being in the paper.

In Dayton no one would want to see me. They thought I was weird. Am I really? I prefer teenagers, eighteen or nineteen. If it's a masochist thing, I prefer adult black men. That's deviant sex, I guess, but I enjoy it anyway. Before, I was depressed about it, thinking it was wrong, from what people like psychiatrists were telling me at the clinic. When I got arrested with a younger person and they said it, I believed them. Now who cares? I know it's not normal, but it doesn't bother me to the point of killing myself.

People put things in your head. When you're arrested, cops tell you that you're crazy, you're sick. After people read it in the paper, they call you and say you should be locked up like an animal. In the paper, they write down your whole name and address. They might as well give your phone number, too, and save people the trouble of looking it up themselves. You'll get threatening phone calls for a month saying you're sick, and you'll start believing it. Then one guy I talked to said that as long as you like doing it, and you're not hurting anyone, do it.

In Spain, everyone looks the other way. I was in a little

village, three hundred people. I saw a man go in with a boy. They didn't make a big stink out of it. The old people don't want to believe it exists, and the young people don't care. They wouldn't call the police, they'd simply throw you out of the village. I'm not saying it's good, but if a guy is shot in the street there and fifty people saw the whole thing, nobody says a word. Here they'd die to get in front of a TV camera . . .

In Ohio, the reason I didn't go to jail is, first, because the judge liked me. And then, the prisons were overcrowded, so overcrowded; they would put a murderer there before me, you know. So in a way if you're getting busted in Ohio, there's less chance you're going to go to jail. Not if it's your first time. In Iowa forget it. [Laughs.] They'd construct a new jail for you.

Jail isn't worth the crime, even if it's ripping off a million dollars. It's the same thing with sex, which is the worst crime that you can commit, as far as jailmates go, especially with children. I'd rather go to jail as a rapist than a pedophile. Your survival chances are greater. The only reason I wasn't killed was because a lot of the guards were Spanish and I'm Spanish. Otherwise they would have kicked my ass right there. If I was given a choice between going to jail or taking the drug, I'd take the drug any day —although not the high dosage.

Jail changed me quick. It's a good idea for someone to go to jail. I don't mean go and stay there, just to see what it's like. In jail it's an honor to have killed a cop. You're a hero. It isn't a secret. But a pedophile is different. The inmates will kill you. They hate you for what you've done. They have a funny sense of morality. Kill someone and they'll love you. That's the way they are in America.

The doctors think that pedophilia is wrong. That using kids for that purpose will hurt them. They're right in that point. There's a lot of pedophiles who use kids and manipulate them into having sex. But they're wrong in thinking that there aren't kids who enjoy it. Lots of times, kids come on to men. They just want money. They get it from older men and go out to buy cocaine with it. They don't go to school. The pedophiles are like a welcome mat. They get stepped on. One kid bought a moped with the money from a regular guy. When he broke it, he demanded another one. The guy got it for him, because he wanted the sex.

In a city like Chicago there's always a hustler for a pedophile. Kids don't look at it that way because they don't hang out on the street anymore. They have enough customers. They can just go to their homes now. They don't want to think they're doing anything gay because they despise faggots. But they shut up, because the older man is paying them. In Dayton, there are no hustlers for a pedophile, so pedophiles have to take a chance. I wouldn't have gotten caught in Chicago if I had sex with a fifteen-year-old when I was seventeen. In Dayton, it becomes the crime of the century.

I'm in favor of treating twelve- or thirteen-year-olds. They're starting to do that now. They're having another clinic with twelve-year-old offenders. There's an article in the paper about it. Just read the last paragraph: " 'There's now no treatment for adolescent offenders in this state, and I think it essential that we have one,' the doctor told them. 'That's how you stop crime.' " I agree with them, in that if they catch sex offenders at an early age, they can be helped. If they're going to go through a life of going to jail, it'd be worth it for them to change it.

I had the cops come up to my house when I was eleven. I exposed myself in front of girls in my neighborhood, the same age as me. They told me I was not to do it again. At that point I should have received help. I knew it wasn't normal, but I didn't know it was wrong, either. I could have sex with a girl right now, but to me, exposing myself is a higher thing.

Still, I'd rather control my sex drive for five years, instead of having a heart attack every time the doorbell rings, thinking it could be the cops. Once they have your picture, then any time a crime happens, they'll show your picture among others. I'm in constant jeopardy of being arrested.

State of Ohio	Sheriff's Department
Affidavit	Case Complaint No. 92

Arthur F. Dillon being duly sworn, deposes and says:

"I am 13 years old. I am giving this voluntary statement to Deputy Mary C. Graham of the Sheriff's Department at my residence at about 10:30 P.M. in the presence of my mother Abigail Dillon.

"Deputy Graham came to my house at about 10:20 P.M. and said she had pictures to show me. She told me to look at nine pictures, numbered 1 through 9. They were in a clear plastic photo page.

"I looked at the pictures for about a minute or so and recognized number 7 as the man who has been harassing me. I am sure that picture number 7 is the man. I put my initials on the back of that picture."

Two months ago, I got arrested on a false charge of harassment. People read in the paper what I did two or three years ago. They wanted me out of the neighborhood. They got a boy to say that I attacked him in the park at night and threw him down and threatened to kill him. I never met him in my life, but people across the street constantly threatened me and called me names, like "faggot." They had the boy call the cops and make a complaint. He made up a whole bunch of lies. He said he didn't recognize my face, but recognized my voice from three years ago. He says I had harassed his little brother then, when my passport proves that I was in Spain.

State of Ohio   Sheriff's Department
Complaint/Information   Case Complaint No. 92

I, Deputy Graham, the Complainant herein, a Deputy Sheriff of the Sheriff's Department at Dayton, Ohio, Accuse José Torres, the Defendant in this action, and charge that on or about the 12th day of August, 1985, at about 9:50 o'clock in the evening, said Defendant did commit the violation of Harassment contrary to the provisions of Section 240.25 sub 1 of the Penal Law of the State of Ohio by intentionally and unlawfully harassing another person by shoving and otherwise subjecting him to physical contact.

To wit: at the above date, time, and location, defendant Torres ran out of some bushes and jumped Arthur Dillon in Sunset Park. He pushed and pulled him to the ground, causing him to strike his face on the ground. He grabbed him by the back of the neck, pulled his face off the ground, and threatened to kill him if he saw him there again.

All contrary to the provisions of the statute in such case made and provided.

Complainant's source of information and grounds for belief being the sworn Affidavit of Arthur F. Dillon, attached hereto and made a part thereof, and the investigation of this writer.

WHEREFORE I REQUEST THAT CRIMINAL PROCESS BE ISSUED TO COMPEL THE DEFENDANT TO ANSWER THE AFORESAID ACCUSATION.

Affidavit   Case Complaint No. 92

"*On Wednesday evening August 12, 1985, at about 9:50 P.M., I was walking home from a friend's house. I*

---

was walking across the ballfield in Sunset Park. A man came out from some trees. As he ran at me, he grabbed my shirt near the neck and pushed me to the ground into some mud. I hit my nose on the ground. He grabbed me by the back of my neck and pulled my face up. I started struggling and he told me something like, 'If I ever see you around here again, you're dead.' He then left me and I ran away.

"Although I couldn't see him clearly because it was dark, I recognized his voice and his physical appearance because I've had other problems with him. Last August I saw him walking on Marrow Road. He stopped me and asked me for directions to MacDonald's. I showed him to MacDonald's, and when we got there he said he would give me a couple of bucks if I would go into the bathroom with him, and after he was done he would give me more money. I ran away.

"Around 2½ to 3 weeks ago the same man followed me in a car as I was riding my bicycle in the area of Bear Terrace and Gramercy Drive. I have also seen him around my school during after-school activities, and around the neighborhood.

"The car he was driving when he followed me was a dark blue car with horizontal yellow door-strips. The man was about 19 to 20 years old. He is about 6 feet tall with a large build. He has dark, ear-length hair, droopy eyes, a large nose, and thick lips. He seems kind of mentally slow. He has a low voice and he talks slow. He has poor posture and his shoulders are hunched over.

"While I was describing him to Deputy Graham, my brother Jeremy said the description sounded like a man that harassed him about 3 years ago. The neighborhood kids call him 'Charlie.' My brother said he lived on Glassboro Parkway. Deputy Graham took my brother and me to Glassboro Parkway so my brother could point

> out the house. I recognized one of the cars in the drive-
> way as the one that the man was driving during the day
> he followed me. I have also seen him in that car with a
> lady with red hair.
> "I know that the meaning of perjury is to tell a lie
> while under oath. I know that false statements made
> herein are punishable as a Class A Misdemeanor pur-
> suant to the Penal Law of the State of Ohio. I have read
> this statement and I swear that it is the truth to the best
> of my knowledge and recollection."

I told my lawyer to tape my voice and see if he could identify my voice among other voices, and that's when they dropped the charges. It was a set-up. So now I'm suing them.

I left the city at the same time. This was in Dayton. It's a small town, and they hate any crime that has to do with sex. I would never say anything against Russia after this shit. [Laughs.] It was only a misdemeanor, but I had to stay in jail because I couldn't get any bail. Getting arrested invalidates probation. A murderer could get bailed out before I could. That's why I'm suing them. They say I threw the kid on the ground, on his face and nose, but there were no bruises on him. How can you throw two hundred pounds on a ninety-pound kid and have no scratches or anything? He said I threatened to kill him. Another lie. The cops could only press harassment. You know what that is? It's like a traffic-ticket charge, that's all. It's less than a misdemeanor. If they say I hit him, why didn't they press assault? There was no proof, that's why. They had to get me for something. They were fair about that. They wished they did have something. They hate me, the police.

And my mother had diabetes and almost ended up in the hospital with a coma. Some hell of a practical joke.

These people weren't that clean themselves. A family of

black people tried to move in, okay? And these white people, they go to church half the day Sunday, they believe in God and all that bullshit. Well, they come out and they threaten these black folks unless they move. They spray-paint their house to get them the hell out of there. They go door-to-door like the Klan.

If it were not for these people, I wouldn't have had to live like that, sitting in jail for thirteen days like an animal. The first week the jails were so full, I stayed in a "galley," they call it. You never saw the sun. Lights on twenty-four hours a day. Then they moved me upstairs where there's *this* much room to walk. Unbelievable. I got claustrophobia. But you learn to deal with it, or you go crazy. One day I got sick because they keep the air conditioner on so high, you're uncomfortable and cold. I got the flu and a fever. So I hid under the covers to keep myself warm. I was shivering. The deputy came by and told me I was locked in twenty-four hours for being under my covers during the daytime! They didn't care if I was sick or not. That's America!

I have to get the hell out of this country. But I'm still on probation. I've got to stay the whole five years. I'll just play it safe. Once you've been in jail, you can wait.

But here in this city, in America, you have so many opportunities. I'd go to the Bus Terminal and pick someone up. There's lots of gay people there. They could be seventeen, eighteen, mostly Puerto Ricans. I'd go down to the warehouses. You just climb the fence and do a masochist act. You know: I'd play the role of a slave, they'd order me to blow them, that type of thing. But I'd be in complete control. I'm not into that stuff like heavy S&M. It's more psychological, the way I like it. I enjoy doing that a lot. It's dangerous, you could pick up the wrong person.

You see, if you wanted me to get arrested, you could just lie. You'd just call the police and tell them I was following this kid right here in the street, and they'd get an "order of protection." I have to stay away from them.

This ain't a free country. Not the way they make it to be, it's not. You can't have sex with whoever you want. You don't even own a house because you've got to go on paying taxes on your property. In Spain you only pay your taxes once, and that's it. Here all you do is watch TV all day. There, in Spain, the food is fresh, there's hardly any cars, it's beautiful. I wouldn't expose myself, because there are so few people. I would get married and settle down, have my own kids. Not for sex, either. I'd take vacations, go to the Philippines . . .

I'm still capable of having sex with girls, you know. I don't really need that pedophile stuff anymore.

9
Deter

"**H**ow do you talk to children when they first come to see you?" I asked the lab technician.

"Well, I say, 'We're going to talk to you about private things, things that are sexual. They may embarrass you. You may feel a little bit nervous or anxious.' We kind of prepare them for it. They might get upset when they listen to some of the homosexual tapes, so I tell them, 'You may like some of the tapes and some you may not.' At the end I tell them that everything they've been exposed to is against the law."

"Did they have any idea what you were going to do with them?"

"They'd been told twice. In the interview, they were shown the device that measures the penis. In the lab, I explain it to them again: 'When you strain the gauge, it records an erection on the machine.' "

"What's their reaction to the machines?"

"They don't react. They're very quiet. Once in a while they might just shake their head. A majority of our kids have low IQ's, so they're pretty slow. Some kids come here who can't read sentences. It's difficult to tell what's going on in their heads."

"It must be a shock, being thrown into these machines."

"Oh yes, no doubt about that. I try to make it as easy as possible. Our door to the lab is a cold-looking metal door, and I tell them, 'I know this looks like a refrigerator, but it isn't so bad. The walls are thick so you won't have anyone disturb you while you're in there.' The door cannot be locked. If they feel claustrophobic, they can leave. I do not shut off the lights; a lot of kids are afraid of the dark."

"None of the children resist treatment?"

"We've run about one hundred fifty boys, and only two just outright refused. Some of the boys are fascinated by the procedure. Very few are so scared that they *look* scared. They may be scared inside, but they don't show anything."

"How long have you been treating juvenile sex offenders?"

"We started two years ago. Programs are springing up all over the United States. Most of them use a family-therapy approach, but we believe the youth themselves should learn control over their wrongful behavior."

"How different is it from the adult program?"

"We shortened the sessions. It's difficult for youths to sit anywhere for an hour. And then, the adults had a long-established pattern of deviant sexual behavior. These kids are just starting."

"Do they recognize that they did something wrong?"

"No. They won't admit that they've engaged in deviant behavior."

"How do you know that they have, then?"

"All our boys have been arrested. They're reported by an adult, usually the mother of the victim. Some of them are incest kids, engaging in sex with their sister; their own mothers reported them. The judge doesn't want to send them off to prison, so they're put on probation pending treatment. Some may have been in a holding cell for a few days. We make contact through the probation officer—many of our kids don't have phones. Probation officers really do care, and they keep an eye on them. But they have case loads of sixty or eighty youths."

"What's the children's background?"

"They're homeless. Their parents may be in jail because of abuse. That sort of thing. Or, they are orphans who live in 'group homes,' which are permanent residences for eight to twelve kids, ages ten to eighteen, sometimes younger. Group homes are their homes. They are run by a couple trained in dealing with children. Charity organizations, like Catholic Charities, or the Jewish Board of Family and Children Services, operate a lot of them throughout the city. It's not an easy environment. So those are the boys we're getting in here. About 90 percent are minority."

"Do you treat any girl offenders?"

"Girl offenders? No, I have never seen one. I have heard of three in twelve years. It doesn't mean that women don't commit sexual crimes. They do. But this is a big city and the numbers are not there."

"Adults had a different background than adolescents?"

"Adults were mostly caucasian. If you're white and if you have the money, you go the mental-health route. You get a good attorney who pleads your case and you get some kind of therapy. When you're poor, black, or hispanic, you wind up in the criminal-justice route, like kids in this program. It's a more violent group because these are city kids. We teach them that they should never force sex on anybody. What would you do, we ask them, if you were with a girl who had agreed to be sexual, and then changed her mind. 'Well,' they say, categorically, 'I wouldn't go on.' And we say, 'That's very good.' Then they say, 'I would punch her out for putting me in that position to begin with.' We didn't hear that with the adult sample."

"And do they agree to the treatment?"

"We read them a detailed consent form which explains that we will be asking them questions about their sexual behavior."

"Do they understand the terms?"

"Oh yes."

"And they cooperate?"

"They're not really trusting us too much. We find that after they're a few months into treatment they're a little more willing to admit that they actually did the behavior, which may have been fondling a little girl, or touching her, or having sex with her."

"How young is the little girl?"

"The typical range is from six to twelve."

"And fondling younger children, that's criminal?"

"Oh yes. The law says that it is criminal if you touch the private parts of a minor—a minor is described as five years younger than the adolescent. Yes, you cannot touch them, genitals, that sort of thing. It's against the law, and it's considered an assault."

"Do they engage in anything more violent than fondling?"

"Some of them engage in penetration—anal, vaginal penetration. That's a felony. I'm not sure whether or not fondling is a felony. I don't think it is."

"Your youth offenders are pretty young themselves."

"They're thirteen to eighteen. Those sixteen or over get charged as adults in court. The ones who go to jail raped girls their own age or adult women. If the behavior is not violent, they're more likely to get a probation. Virtually all of our kids are at puberty."

"How do adolescents compare with adults in the lab?"

"When we first started running adolescents, we thought they would get more response than adults, because the material might be more novel to them. Older men have pretty much seen everything. However, since they're all minority kids, they've seen a considerable amount of pornography, so they don't get that much arousal in the lab."

"What happens when they get an erection in the lab?"

"By and large, the adolescents will tend to say that they have no erections when they have a lot, especially with the right cue. They won't admit that they get aroused to a little girl. There's a societal constraint to that."

"How old is the little girl in the picture?"

"About six years old."

"Is she dressed?"

"She's naked."

"Anything more specific?"

"No. It's very hard to get that sort of picture. If they molested a two-year-old girl, we can't be that specific. We have only pictures ranging in age from four all the way up to adults. They come from a person in the Middle West who is licensed to dispense this kind of material for research. Child pornography magazines used to be available in New York in the seventies, but since they've tightened up the laws, you really have to go underground to buy them. We tried a few years ago meeting someone in an alley, and sometimes that can get dangerous. So we got them through official channels, which also provides standardized assessments for researchers using similar pictures around the country."

"Can you describe the typical child picture you use?"

"It won't be hard-core pornography. The child will just be standing there. There will be frontal nudity. Or she will be lying down. Her legs might be spread over a little bit, but not all the way out. She will not have her finger in her vagina, or anything like that. She will not be performing sexual acts with anybody else."

"Could it look like a family picture?"

"It's one person per picture, a sole one stimulus."

"I meant, could a father have taken that kind of picture?"

"Oh no. Although one way to get pictures is to look through nudist magazines for pictures of families and just crop for the little girl. We did get a couple of pictures that way."

"Can you use the set of pictures that were developed for pedophiles?"

"We can, but our stimulus set for adolescents is different because of the ethical problem. We didn't include, for instance, sadistic kinds of acts involving razor blades, or victims tied up. Very few of our boys are aware of sadistic pornography. Children are more impressionable. We are careful not to expose them to things they might want to imitate."

"In the verbal cues, do you take into account the language difference?"

"We didn't want to use street language because it changes practically every three months. We got around that by making the language as simple as possible. With adults we would say, 'You're masturbating that boy.' Here we say, 'You're touching that boy, you're touching him where he doesn't want you to.' We don't ever use slang terms like 'cock'; they would sound ridiculous if they were not used anymore, and that would ruin the tape."

"You never designate the organ explicitly?"

"No, we don't. The tape for adolescents isn't specific. They've got to put themselves in the scene. With the adults' tapes, we say, 'You're putting your penis in her vagina.' Well, we found that some of the boys would orally sodomize a person, and some anally, and others vaginally. So we just say, 'You're putting it in her, or in him.' And they can imagine whatever orifice is arousing to them. We might say 'breasts,' that we might say. We might use the word 'penis' because they pretty much know what a penis is."

"But how do you know what you're testing?"

"It doesn't make a difference if they really raped anally or vaginally. What we are testing is the amount of coercion, as well as the age of the victim. What's important is that it was a child and that the behavior wasn't consensual."

"How long are your descriptions?"

"For the satiation, it is one sentence. For the evaluation, just two-minute tapes. For instance, I play them a tape describing voyeuristic acts: They're walking home at night and they look in a window and see a woman getting out of the shower. They stop and stare. She's totally naked. They're watching her and getting really hard. She has big breasts and she's touching them and massaging them. She looks at herself in the mirror while they're watching her. Like that.

"Peeping-tomism is a crime, but for someone to get aroused looking through windows might be a normal thing. We just wanted to see if kids would get aroused with tapes like that. So far, it's unclear: half of them do and half don't. But the tapes are pretty much all in that vein, and a lot of imagery-producing statements."

"What happens after they listen to a tape?"

"After each one I ask them if it felt arousing in their mind. They don't often know what 'arousing' means, so I explain: 'Did it feel sexual in your mind?' Then I ask them how much erection they've got. If they don't know what 'erection' means, I might ask, 'Is your penis hard?' or I'll just say, 'Is it hard?' "

"The satiation tapes are done at home?"

"No. We found that they don't make them at home. And then with the adults most of the tape recorders and tapes we passed out were stolen. So now they are done in the lab. The boys wear the strain gauge while they look at the picture and they repeat the phrase over and over. We want to know if they get an erection while they look at the picture. Normally they don't, because the act of speaking prevents them from it."

"They always repeat the same sentence?"

"The same sentence, for twenty minutes. The sentence might be, 'I'm feeling this girl's body.' It's something short. I tell them in advance that it's going to be boring for twenty minutes."

"You tell them that *in advance?*"

"Yes. And I tell them it's good that it's boring, and it *should* be boring, and that if it's boring, that means it's working. I really set them up to be bored."

"So they get bored to the picture of a little girl lying on a bed? What's the point?"

"What is it?"

"Yes. What is the point of being satiated to a little girl lying on the bed?"

"They're being satiated to telling the little girl to lie on the bed."

"Oh, so it's an order—'Lie on the bed.' "

"Yes. The statement that they might repeat over and over is, 'I am telling this girl to lie on the bed.' It's usually a statement involving some degree of coercion, feeling the girl's body, holding her down."

"Are they allowed to introduce variations, or is it

strictly like being asked to copy fifty times the same line at school?"

"That's the same principle. The more variation they do, the least satiation. It has to be something that's repeated over and over again."

"You don't have any ethical problem asking them to masturbate?"

"We're not asking them to masturbate. We modified the satiation. All they do is repeat over and over what it is that they did."

"That's a major change, isn't it? To do masturbatory satiation without masturbation! Is repetition enough to do the job?"

"Oh, the masturbation is highly effective, but this works too. The problem with masturbation is getting consent from the parents. So many parents did not consent that we had to take masturbation out of our procedure. And we've shown that when they're tested again with the audio-tapes and the pictures, there's less arousal to the deviant target while it doesn't change that much with the adult targets. So the effect is specific. What's important is that they're hearing what it is that they did. When you've got a sixteen-year-old repeating that he did something to a four-year-old, he realizes, I think, that it's inappropriate. And it becomes aversive because I'm right there listening."

"Are you trying to shame them or convince them rationally? I thought the whole purpose of the treatment was to create an immediate visceral reaction to the idea. Isn't that how satiation is supposed to work?"

"When Bill Marshall first described it, he distinguished two components, one being the repetition and the other being the punishment of having to masturbate post-ejaculation. We're finding that the repetition appears to be effective in and of itself."

"You mean that each time they see a little girl, they're going to repeat their lines?"

"You don't have to repeat them. You can learn very quickly how to inhibit arousal through some mental gymnastics, if you want."

"Didn't you say that they are not especially bright?"

"You don't have to be bright to do that. It is very simplistic."

"What's amazing is that there should be a satiation effect through verbal repetition only."

"Well, there's certainly satiation to that particular sentence. Now we don't have any evidence that the phrase that I am giving them is that arousing to begin with. It's just a phrase."

"Can't you test the phrase in the lab?"

"No, I can't do it. No one can repeat one single phrase and get aroused to it. It has to be part of a larger story. The only way to really do it is have the kids develop verbal fantasies in the lab."

"Don't you do that with them?"

"No. The one reason we don't want to do that is because they didn't have any fantasy to begin with."

"What do you mean?"

"None of them admit that they had deviant fantasies, fantasies that they masturbate to at night, or something that they think about. They're pretty much *never* willing to admit that they actually do that."

"Are you sure they fantasize at all?"

"We don't know. It's just a guess."

"Is fantasizing unavoidable?"

"It is a fact that 99 percent of men masturbate and that virtually every time someone masturbates, there's a fantasy associated with it—unless they're watching a pornographic movie or looking at a pornographic magazine."

"But these boys are pretty young. How can you be sure that they ever masturbated?"

"That's another interesting thing. A lot of the kids will say that they never, never, never masturbated before. Whether or not that's true is a matter of debate. Some deny it in the initial interview, but when it's discussed later on in treatment—weeks, months later—they will admit that they've done it and will continue to do it. It's not something a boy likes to talk about with an adult, especially the first time they meet him. It's something that's extremely private, something that they hide from their parents. It's one of the only experiences they have had that no one knows about, especially if they are fourteen or thirteen and recently discovered it. I have to think back to when I was thirteen; I wouldn't have wanted to talk about that with anybody, especially when you've been involved in a sexual offense which you don't want to talk about at all."

"What about the fantasy, then? You're supposed to treat fantasies; how can you do that if you're not sure they have any?"

"We almost have to guess that they have fantasies."

"And the fantasy that you ask them to repeat in the lab, where does it come from?"

"We give it to them. We use something very general, so the person can make up his own fantasy as it goes along. Each session involves a different fantasy."

"Which you set up for them."

"Yes. I will use their case history to guide me, and for the rest . . ."

"You leave that to their imagination, and to chance."

"Yes."

"At least this says something about adolescent sexuality. Isn't it more diffuse, less centered on genitality?"

"Yes. It's probably more diffused. The fantasies men engage in are based on experience and develop through time. Likewise in a sexual deviation. These kids have not developed specific preferences for, say, eight-year-old girls. A lot of the assaults occur while they're baby-sitting, so it might have to do with the spontaneous arousal that adolescents get, and here's a convenient target. Where it becomes dangerous for future targets is when they start fantasizing about the young child while masturbating to that fantasy. We have no way to assess whether or not this happens, because the kids will not admit that they fantasize about small children. We don't want to develop verbal deviant fantasies in kids, as it is done in private practice with adults. If we could do that with kids, we could say that a certain part of the fantasy provokes a tremendous erection; then we could have them satiate it by saying the thing over and over, and test it later on to make sure there is no more arousal. But it's unethical to develop deviant verbal fantasies in kids."

"So what you're doing in the lab is just like a shot in the dark. You may be satiating them on something that's not arousing."

"That's very possible."

"And this doesn't bother you?"

"No, because it's the best we can do. We can't get inside their heads, so we give them a fantasy which may or may not be deviant for them. The fact of the matter is, if they don't fantasize, then what we're doing is preventing them from fantasizing in the future. It could be seen as a preventive measure, nipping something in the bud, so to speak. There's a strong possibility that we're interrupting a deviant chain of events that might be happening here."

"Or somewhere else, or not at all."

"Frankly, how it generalizes to the outside world is unclear. You don't know. Our only measure is recidivism, if they get arrested again. But they could be out there offending and not get arrested. So what you do is try to imitate life as much as possible. Of course, it's a poor imitation. Ideally you would have a deviant target walk into the lab and sit on their lap, but of course you can't do that. If you wanted to treat the real-life situation, you'd go with them to their house, measure their erections right there, with a little girl who is naked sitting with them on the couch. That would be the way to do it."

One More Time

**Now we've done with sex
where we gonna go?**

—Kathy Acker

I can still remember the amazement (and excitement) I felt when I realized for the first time what the new treatment of sexual deviance was about: *Give 'em more of it!* The idea could only have come from a dark humorist—Kafka or William Burroughs.

It must have taken a lot of thought to come up with this simple solution: satiation. Until recently, aversion therapy was the only psychiatric treatment deemed effective, and it was a rather distasteful project. Coupling pleasure with pain certainly manages to deter deviance, but the idea of shocking a transvestite out of his wits as he's cross-dressing, or making a homosexual vomit with each erection is not something one would really boast about. In a civilized society, coercion must remain invisible. Crime victims are on the front page of every morning paper, but death row remains off-limits. There's something obscene or tactless about legal violence.

Dr. José Delgado, a "bioideologist" from Yale University, thought of implanting electrodes directly into patients' brains. The offender's bursts of assaultive behavior, he argued, can be inhibited as they are about to occur. If remote-controlled cerebral stimulation can freeze a cat in the middle of a jump, even stop a fighting bull in full charge, it should be possible to prevent an individual from flashing open his coat, or a rapist from jumping his victim. The technique is certainly cleaner than "open brain surgery"—read: lobotomy—which massively destroys nervous structures. Still, there's something rather sinister about sticking electrodes in someone's brain. The best controls by far—those that at least leave our conscience at peace—are invisible. Ideally they should be one with the individual himself.

The haunting image of the bull stopped dead by an invisible switch already stands, monumental, at the threshold of another era. Physical coercion has run its course. Talking is now the punishment.

Sexuality isn't just repressed, Michel Foucault asserts in *The History of Sexuality*; rather, it is "expressed" everywhere, on every occasion, and this deeply affects the vision we have of social control. We are forced to speak about sex "in public and in private, to one's parents, one's educators, one's doctors, to those one loves. . . ." Foucault's description of the Victorians as a "confessing society" meshes uncannily with contemporary society—especially America—where the "talking cure" has become an unconscious reflex in daily life. With a wave of the hand, Foucault's thesis dismissed and demolished the theories of repression which had been developed over a decade by the Frankfurt School, beginning with Wilhelm Reich and culminating with Herbert Marcuse.

In a seminal essay, "About the Concept of the 'Dangerous Individual' in Nineteenth-Century Legal Psychiatry," published in 1975, Michel Foucault tells of a French rapist who refused to speak to his judges. "Defend yourself!" one of the jurors finally blurted out, exasperated. Power is on the side of those who remain silent. Only victims talk. His lawyer's reaction was all the more amazing: "Can you condemn to death," he argued, *"a person you don't know?"*

Two centuries ago this argument would have been met with incredulity. Justice dealt with the crime, not with the criminal. Later, in the wake of new humanitarian concerns, the view arose that violence no longer canceled the deed, but rather added to it. To rise above vengeance and modulate the sentence the law had to take into account the defendant's psychology. Crime became a "symptom," and the administration of justice a therapy of the social body. Knowledge about the offender's mind became inextricably bound to the legal proceeding. This new system, mixing science with restraint, is what Foucault called the "power-knowledge" complex.

Foucault's study on sexuality is an offshoot of his interest in nineteenth-century criminality, in which he found welded together the practice of confession and the birth of the power-knowledge system. How do you protect society from the risk of criminality represented by a particular personality? The notion of "dangerousness' (which has no legal status) gave psychiatry an opportunity to infiltrate the law. Dipping into the maze of the individual's mind, psychiatrists managed to impose their expertise on the modern penal system. Caught in an endless spiral, both institutions kept hovering uneasily between retribution and rehabilitation.

The present configuration of the American medicolegal system, however, is far removed from the nineteenth century. Over the past twenty years American judicial philosophers have tried to offset the inequalities that once permitted broad judicial "discretion." In a strange amalgamation, egalitarian discourse and legalistic concerns joined hands in a powerful reformist movement. Civil-rights proponents have paradoxically dehumanized justice, advocating the return to a "blind" system of punishment. Contrary to public perception, it is rare today to see psychiatrists discussing the delinquent's psychology with the jury. (In any event, most cases are now plea-bargained.)

A further change away from individualism in treatment has occurred within the therapeutic community itself. While psychoanalysis is still the banner of the profession, more pragmatic and "democratic" *technologies of behavior* have been implemented everywhere. Coupled with the return to a retributive conception of punishment, these technologies are a powerful challenge to the "just individualization" of crime which Foucault put at the heart of the power-knowledge system, and at the foundation of his own problematization of sexuality.

The treatment administered at the clinic for sexual deviance is the evaluative branch of this new technology. Sex therapists don't analyze the character or motivations of the offender. Identifying arousal patterns as a mechanic checks an engine, they merely search for the mental dysfunction, hoping to remove it painlessly, with the appropriate tools.

Proponents of the technologies of behavior claim that they can determine the real causes of human action and reduce their negative consequences. Punishment is obsolete, claims B. F. Skinner, the outspoken proponent of behavioral methods. Control should be exerted *directly* by the social environment to make sure that "behavior likely to be punished seldom or never occurs."

Behaviorism represents a radical departure from the ethos of the free individual. Unlike analysis, its methods yield fast results. But there's more to behaviorism's techniques than recipes and instant gratification. Through them we glimpse the kind of culture they are trying to promote. When Skinner, pushing individual adjustment to the extreme, advocates going "beyond freedom and dignity," he is not so much challenging Western values as revealing them for what they are.

Behaviorism marks the end of the "humanist" era, and with it, of the type of "productive" power analyzed by Foucault. The present volume actually could be read as a postmodern update to the "end of man" that Foucault, rewriting Nietzsche, boldly proclaimed in 1969. The "good news," actually, didn't address man as such, but the divine image he had invented for himself in the nineteenth century and handed down to existentialist philosophy. The idea that individual consciousness could be the origin and foundation of truth, freedom, and history was finally losing all credibility. Human subjectivity, however, remained intact, and this is precisely what behavioral therapies, answering Foucault's call with a vengeance, are now busy exterminating.

Setting out to write a political history of the production of truth in our societies, Foucault realized that sexuality, shrouded, it would seem, in secrecy, has been taken as emblematic of what is most hidden in our individuality. We see this in Freud, whose inherited Judeo-Christian model equated the search for truth with the confession of one's sins. But what if the ritual of confession had outlived its function, sexuality now being fully externalized? What if the discourse on sex had no more truth to deliver, only filling the air with an improbable babble simulating sociability?

The dazzling transformation in contemporary mores can be best epitomized by the changing of attitudes toward masturbation. Witness the frenzy over children's "self-abuse" which swept over Europe in the nineteenth century. (This phenomenon is, ironically, replicated in the current campaign against child abuse.) Parents were warned against this "deadly vice" which was decimating the young. Documents of the time describe the gothic contraptions that were routinely applied to the sinful parts: chains, locks, straps, bonds, bandages, straightjackets. There was no limit to parents' tender care: not only were children checked in bed and spied on in dormitories, but we have accounts of a family doctor who reported cauterizing two little girls' clitorises with hot iron to cool off their "heinous habit."

Today masturbation has not only ceased to be guilty and secretive, it is openly recommended—even taught—as an indispensible tool for sex therapy and a means of enhancing sexual experience: remember the spate of "how-to" masturbation handbooks of the seventies. "Masturbation, fornication, defecation: serious words from his childhood, representing activities to be pondered before being indulged in," writes Julian Barnes in his novel *Before She Met Me*. "Nowadays it was all wanking and fucking and shitting, and no one thought twice about any of them." Masturbatory satiation (ponderous words) does better still. It manages to turn wanking into a punishment.

Modern societies have "dedicated themselves to speaking of sex *ad infinitum*, while exploiting it as *the* secret," Foucault wrote. But this thesis presumes that speaking of sex is still tied to a search for truth. In fact, Dr. Sachs seems closer to the current version of reality when he declares: "Oh, I tell my patients exactly what the treatment is. There's no secret here."

In Dr. Sachs's treatment everything that concerns the patient's "paraphilias" is discussed openly, even technically, without the habitual silence of the psychoanalyst or the professional secrecy of the doctor. There is a good reason: verbalization "desensitizes" sex. No longer valued as a secret, sex talk infuses the ambiance of sexuality in the clinic as well as in the outside world.

Today confidential information is often revealed at first sight, on the slightest pretext, as if telling everything at once was the natural thing to do, the prerequisite to a friendly encounter. I remember sitting on an airplane and overhearing the conversation of two people who had just met at JFK. By the time we landed in San Francisco, they had no more secrets to share. Actually I would hesitate calling the exhaustive report they exchanged on each other's intimate lives "secret." Maybe for lack of other socializing rituals Americans use sex to talk about themselves, which seems to be their prime occupation; their indentity is apparently so fragile or elusive that it constantly needs checking, as one feels one's wallet to make sure it's still there. Sexuality no longer expresses any truth; it is simply, to borrow Erving Gofman's formula, the presentation of self in everyday life.

Secrets that can be told are not secrets at all. They are some kind of *social secretion*. A woman once phoned me to arrange to see the New York apartment I was subletting. She insisted she had to see it before she and her boyfriend left town to spend the weekend in Long Island. "My boyfriend is a lawyer," she said. "We've been together for a few years, but we've had some problems. Our sex life hasn't been that great lately. Actually it's lousy. I'm hoping that moving to a new place might help us get it together again . . ." I agreed to show her the apartment at the time she requested—and then she canceled the appointment just a few minutes before she was due to arrive. I knew all about her private life though I had not even seen her face. "That's the way of all secrets as soon as they're aired in public," Céline wrote. "What's really awesome in us and on the earth, in the sky maybe, has not yet been said. We won't rest until everything has been said, once and for all, then we'll remain silent, we won't be afraid of being mute. That will be it."

Robert Stoller also gives secrecy a primary importance in the sexual process. Without the sense of danger and mystery, he writes in *Perversion, the Erotic Form of Hatred*, sexual arousal turns into indifference and boredom. One is reminded of Dr. Sachs's description of the "extremely boring life" of the typical married fellow. While deploring the fact, Stoller recognizes that perversion is an indispensible ingredient of "enthusiastic lust." If, as Foucault insisted, modern society is perverse, then postmodernity is *obscene*. Crudely exposing everything sexual, it merely destroys the excitement.

It may have sounded outlandish at first that psychiatrists should prescribe sexual offenders all the sex they can take, and more. But all they do really is administer more massively, and according to some rules, the same kind of "treatment" that's available everywhere. The new technology of sex, as Dr. Sachs recognizes, is "close to the real world," by which he means the consumer world. Could it be then that in the real world as well the intense circulation of sexual signs is satiating sexuality?

There's no need to turn the world into a lab to check on that. "I get fed up with it," complains the sex specialist, to be sure, not a pervert himself. "I talk about sex *all* day long, and it does get to be a drag." His daily exposure to the deviates' diet is enough to put him off sex. New therapists, too, "get satiated very fast." Is there a better confirmation for the "generalizing" effect of the treatment?

Far from being a passive microcosm of society, the sex clinic participates creatively in the engineering of an improved version of humanity: "You have a new person that goes out," asserts the psychiatrist. From a dangerous deviate, the patient ideally becomes a grateful clone. In the process, normality receives a much-needed boost. It can be seen again as a daring adventure—and an enviable promotion. If everyone could only be a deviate, normality would still have a bright future.

But maybe everyone is. Deviate or dysfunctional, the difference isn't that significant, at least in therapeutic terms. Actually—and this came as a revelation—both the reductive and the remedial therapies come from the same source: satiation was first applied to dysfunctions. They also share the same paradoxical premises: controlled abstinence energizes failing desires, while immoderate consumption stems the overflow. Excess and deficit balance themselves out in the new technology of sex, protecting this reusable biosocial construct which, probably out of habit, we keep calling human sexuality. Sex, says Dr. Sachs flatly, is just "an area of observable behavior measurable by instruments."

"The only thing they work with is your penis," complains a patient. This is true enough, but the sex clinic is no "penile colony" for all that. The strange assemblage of high technology, flaccid organs, and hardened dentistry doesn't cut in the flesh the letter of the old law, nor does it reclaim, in a more modernist fashion, the subject's soul ("I feel less remorse for the victim than I did before I came here," marvels a rapist.) Clinging like so many spiders on the patient's anatomy, all the sex machines do is suck information.

Yet they are not after penile measurements, but thoughts that can be verbalized. The technique actually provides its own bold definition of mental processes: "You can never really look inside," Dr. Sachs says, "except in the sexual area—if you assume that *erection equals thought.*"

There is something vaguely obscene (or grotesque) about this desire to penetrate someone else's thoughts by way of his penis. As if the therapist answered the voyeur —or the rapist—in kind. ("What is happening inside?" wonders the sex researcher. "I don't know. But I can hear the words.")

Yes, but whose words are they? Psychiatrists and patients "collaborate" to give deviant sexuality a tangible form. Turning muted desires into articulate fantasies is quite a therapeutic feat; coupled with masturbation, it verges on acrobatics. It's no wonder that, at times, the codes get hopelessly tangled up. "Are those your own words, Jim?" asks Dr. Sachs. "Is that a product of your therapy in the past or is that how you've always felt?" The therapist should know. All along he's been feeding patients his own cues. The trick is to make sex truly reappear (and disappear) when what we're dealing with is not sex itself, but carefully constructed representations of it.

The psychiatrist's effort to search and destroy his elusive objects ends up in self-parody. While the doctor keeps "looking inside," the patient tries to please him by planting in his own head some "seeds of reality." Both would like to believe that they're doing something real, but reality remains slippery. The program for adolescent offenders, however, doesn't even make the pretense of therapeutic subtleties: unable to lay his hands on any fantasy, the therapist squarely dictates to children their "lines," using police transcripts. (Masturbation optional.)

More than masturbation, verbalization—verbal masturbation—is essential to the treatment. The clinic keeps turning sex into discourse. The "elegance" of the technique lies in its vertiginous simplicity. In the new "talking cure," talking is the therapy. The treatment is emblematic for the culture because it answers any possible disruption with the power of verbal exchange. "We're working on communication in the sexual area," recognizes Dr. Sachs. We have not yet acknowledged the violence of enforced communication.

Roman Jakobson, the famous linguist, once attacked angrily the notion of "idiolect." A language spoken by one person only, he declared, is a "perverse fiction." That Jakobson would raise the question of perversion in such a context is fascinating. Linking language and the theory of communication, the linguist explains: "While we speak to a new interlocutor, we always try, deliberately or involuntarily, to discover a common language: whether in order to be appreciated, or simply to make ourselves understood, or else to get rid of the person, we end up using the very terms that he uses. There's no such thing as a private property in the sphere of language; everything is socialized."

Language is indeed a way of relating. Communicating is a social imperative, and expressing oneself a moral obligation. Anything that threatens verbal reciprocity—or any other form of human interaction—is deeply corruptive and should be put under close surveillance. Idiolectic ("antisocial") actions or passions are unacceptable, unless they belong to the pathology of language. Only aphasiacs are allowed to remain silent.

Aphasiacs don't understand the common code. They see it as an "unknown language," if not a "perverse fiction," a refreshing thought which turns the table on normality. Perversions, similarly, allow us to see "normal sex" as a social artifact, and not, as it claims, a "natural phenomenon."

What the clinic dispels, furthermore, is the old humanist idea that communication is meaningful. Its primary function, in fact, has become mechanical: maintaining contact and insuring social cohesion. This is exactly how Dr. Sachs envisions sexuality. For him sex is "a built-in opportunity for closeness." It doesn't have to be sexual, or pleasurable, as long as it socializes.

Ironically, our society makes us believe that sexuality is our dearest secret while at the same time turning it into an instrument of socialization. As Céline perceived, "There comes a time when there are no more secrets, or only those made up by the police." Nature alone, it seems, could have accomplished this miracle of bioengineering: a built-in communication opportunity that could be pleasurable as well. Communication itself is our culture's last ritual, and verbal exchange our ultimate intercourse.

Most of our problems, behaviorists assert, come from "static" in communication. If we could only avoid "cognitive distortions," unnecessary frictions would evaporate and a realm of rational transparency would ensue. "If you don't have any thoughts," assures the therapist, pursuing this line of reasoning, "you don't have any urges." If we all lived in labs, we certainly would have a more optimistic vision of the universe. Irrationalities keep clogging up social conduits; they should be flushed from every area of life. Sexual clinics are a significant part of this grandiose scheme. They "function in communication in the sexual area."

Sexual deviates suffer from a deficit in communication. If they had the necessary skills, wouldn't they love and desire *like anyone else?* These skills can be taught. More meaningful models, more assertive behaviors, more successful techniques of socialization will help smooth out asperities, enhancing in every possible fashion the packaging of the ego. The "pick-up technology" practiced in sex clinics extends this conviction to theater of the absurd.

In the last years of his life Foucault used to say, "Sex is boring." Boredom therapy highlights the curious dilemma of our postmodernity: pleasure, not pain, consumption, not prohibition, have become our punishment. Repetition is the norm, and the cure. Who can truly say that he is living *his own* life? We're all copying lines, as children used to do at school, and as adolescent offenders now do at the clinic. The end of the century is getting closer, and the end of the world remains an open-ended question. But at least we've managed to be through with something: the "secret" of sexuality. Sexuality is no longer repressed, but no longer desirable. It is what's left to be desired when desire amounts to nothing.

As behaviorism finishes off the myth of "humanist" sexuality, it tells us nothing about "perversions," which it treats uniformly. The therapy itself, as Dr. Sachs recognizes, is no different from what is being done everywhere in the "real world." The real-life situation may turn out, after all, to be only a rather poor imitation of the treatment. Whether or not the clinic actually cures or controls sex offenses, or for how long, finally, is not the important issue. Perhaps the simulation of treatment simply answers the fiction of sexuality in our culture.

Love too was a fiction, one of the most formative myths our culture has secreted. With the extenuation of myths and creeds, fictions had to cut closer to the bone. Sexuality assumed love's function: socializing desires. What the therapy reveals in an exemplary fashion is that the physicality of sex, like everything else, has been turned into an abstraction. Those who take it literally are seen as a living anachronism, an embarrassment. Endlessly talked about, tested, and scrutinized, sexuality is now mass-produced as a natural instinct. Collectively "treated," individual sexuality actually self-destructs. Made predictable, satisfaction becomes superfluous. Pleasure turns into a chore, and a bore. Instead of enhancing the deepest mysteries in humankind, it turns us into dogs.

About the Author

Writer, theoretician, and intellectual impresario, Sylvère Lotringer is best known as the founder of *Semiotext[e]*, the influential journal that brought together French post-structuralist theory and the New York avant-garde. Lotringer's interviews with New York artists were anthologized in *New York Art* (Berlin, 1985); his book-length interviews with Paul Virilio and Jean Baudrillard were published as *Pure War* (1983) and *Forget Baudrillard* (1987), and have been translated into several languages. His book on Antonin Artaud will be published in 1988, and he is at work on a novel based on his travels with African nomads. Lotringer, who was a student of Roland Barthes and Lucian Goldman in Paris in the 1960s, is a professor of French literature and philosophy at Columbia University. He lives in New York City.